THERAPY GAMES FOR TEENS

THERAPY GAMES FOR TEENS

150 Activities to Improve Self-Esteem, Communication, and Coping Skills

Kevin Gruzewski, CTRS

CALLISTO PUBLISHING

Published by Callisto Publishing LLC C/O Sourcebooks LLC

P.O. Box 4410, Naperville, Illinois 60567-4410

(630) 961-3900

callistopublishing.com

Printed and bound in China.

1010 27

Much love for my family—BethAnn, Rivers, and Emry—for their support. And props to those professionals using recreation every day as a means to help and heal.

Contents

Introduction

Greetings, fellow therapists, counselors, clinicians, social workers, and parents! My name is Kevin Gruzewski, and I had the pleasure of using recreation as a mode of therapy for almost 20 years. As a Certified Therapeutic Recreation Specialist (CTRS), I saw firsthand the amazing potential recreational activities have for transformation—especially in teens.

I started my career working in a residential facility for adults with developmental disabilities. I quickly learned how important it was to provide and adapt activities to fit the diverse needs of my residents.

A little more than halfway through my recreation therapy career, I switched gears. I took a job as a recreation therapist in a residential drug rehabilitation and mental health setting for adolescent boys. Many of the teens I worked with were from disenfranchised areas of Chicago and tied to gangs and the criminal justice system.

At first, this change was a bit of a culture shock. I was working with teens apprehensive about being placed in treatment and focused on one thing—their discharge date. I faced a learning curve and quite a bit of adapting to fit the diverse backgrounds and motivations of these teens. It wasn't always pretty. I had my fair share of moments being called some very interesting names. Luckily, one of the most effective ways to get through to these boys was using recreational experiences.

Why Recreational Therapy?

According to the National Council for Therapeutic Recreation Certification (NCTRC), recreational therapy "...is a systematic process that utilizes recreation and other activity-based interventions to address the assessed needs of individuals with illnesses and/or disabling conditions as a means to psychological and physical health, recovery, and well-being."

Recreational therapy is about getting to know our clients, discovering their interests, and using these interests to address need areas. When used therapeutically, recreation can provide engaging, teachable moments unlike most other therapy modalities.

Recreational therapy is especially perfect for teens because it harnesses their skills and interests to focus on what's troubling them. For example, an introverted teen who loves to draw or paint has the opportunity to create a piece of art that allows the teen to communicate issues in a more comfortable way.

A great recreational activity can also neutralize defensiveness and allow a teen to open up to new ideas. When this happens, the potential for learning experiences can be amazing—even life-changing. I learned several important lessons for creating activities that resonate with teens.

The most important lesson I learned was to engage the teens. Find topics that are important to them. Allow them to participate in an activity that doesn't necessarily feel like therapy. Encourage them to reach that "flow state," when an activity offers just the right amount of challenge that they lose track of time and place and become immersed. It's not always easy to get and keep a teen engaged. It takes some practice, patience, and a passion to see teens excel during difficult times. But it's certainly worth it when it happens.

I want to use this opportunity to pass on my knowledge and experience to you. Even during the difficult days, I found it very rewarding working with teens. There was something almost magical when they reached an "aha" moment or discovered an insight they never considered before. Recreational activities can help facilitate this.

Why This Book?

If you are like most professionals working with teens or parents raising them, you're juggling all sorts of responsibilities each day. You probably wish you could devote more time to thoughtful activity planning.

Also, you're probably operating on a tight budget. You simply don't have the resources to spend on expensive games or curriculums you aren't sure will work.

This book gives you an opportunity to implement simple group and one-on-one sessions with minimal prep time. Best of all, many of the activities in this book require only easy-to-find supplies that you probably have at your disposal already.

Will you be sacrificing quality with quick prep times and not using a bunch of expensive materials? Absolutely not! As an incredibly busy recreation therapist, I learned how even simple activities can have a profound effect on teens with a variety of challenges if they are done with the teens' specific strengths and needs in mind.

About the Activities

Some of the activities included in this book are my favorite ones that seem to really resonate with teens. Others are evidence-based practices that have been adapted for today's teens.

Teens are a unique breed. Their brains continue to change and mature. At their stage of development, testing boundaries and challenging the established norms are par for the course. The activities in this book help teens let their guard down. They let teens feel like they're more in control and not just getting "preached" to by a therapist or adult who they feel doesn't understand them. It's an opportunity for growth while having fun.

This is the book I wish I had back in the days when I was frantically planning activities. It is filled with practical exercises and activities that meet teens where they are and provide a starting point for change.

How to Use This Book

In this book, you'll get a variety of activities for both group and individual sessions—presented in a simple recipe-like format. The activities cover a lot of ground, like self-exploration, creative expression, team building, developing coping skills, leisure education, and so much more.

Each chapter of this book addresses a topic commonly affecting youths and adolescents, like self-esteem, grief, and bullying. Each topic offers 15 activities separated into three levels. In general, the level breakdown looks like this:

Level 1: gaining a better understanding of the particular topic

Level 2: taking a deeper look at the topic and ways to address it

Level 3: developing coping skills to help teens thrive in everyday life

Although the activity levels help facilitate a deeper understanding of each subject, you don't have to do these activities in order. Every teen comes to therapy with a different skill set. Use the activities you think will most resonate with your teen(s). Meet them where they are in their understanding and coping. Since many issues teens face overlap, you're likely to find appropriate activities in just about any chapter.

I've also included "Pro Tips" with each activity to give you ideas for adapting the activity to the needs of your teen(s). These tips are the result of years of experiences—both good and bad—and will likely help you provide a more meaningful therapy session for your teen(s).

Discussion Questions

The debriefing session after an activity is just as important, if not more important, as the activity itself. The discussion you have after an activity provides learning experiences, insights, and those "aha" moments that will resonate with teens long after the activity is finished.

With each activity, I've offered a few open-ended "Discussion Questions" to help teens put the activity into perspective. Please use these questions as a starting point. Add your own questions as the discussion continues. I truly believe the discussion portion of each activity serves as an important pivotal point where teens can apply what they learned during an activity to their everyday lives.

Ready to get started? I hope this book becomes a treasured resource for you and a source of inspiration for the teen(s) you're serving.

CHAPTER 1

MINDFULNESS

Mindfulness is an awareness of the present moment. Developing this awareness, however, is easier said than done. Fortunately, there are many techniques you can use to practice and teach mindfulness—and some of them can even be fun.

Practicing mindfulness calms the mind, helping us realize that we are not our thoughts, feelings, and sensations—they're just passing through us. This can be especially helpful for teens, who often feel pulled in every direction by peer pressure, family expectations, school, work, and their own goals.

The activities in this chapter are divided into three levels. Introduction to Mindfulness (Level 1) starts with simple exploratory activities to help teens become more aware of their thoughts, feelings, and emotions. Practicing Mindfulness (Level 2) uses proven mindfulness techniques to strengthen their ability to return to a mindful state. Incorporating Mindfulness into Daily Life (Level 3) helps teens incorporate mindfulness into their everyday lives.

What Am I Feeling?

Noticing sensations
in the body

Level 1
Introduction to
Mindfulness

What You'll Need: No materials needed

Duration: 15 minutes

Best for: 1 to 5 people

LEADING THE ACTIVITY

1. Discuss that an important aspect of mindfulness is noticing sensations in the body.

2. Have the teen(s) find a comfortable place to sit for a few minutes, closing their eyes if they choose.

3. After a few deep breaths, invite them to focus on their breath.

4. Ask them to pay attention to any sensations they experience. Tell them to simply notice these sensations, not judge or try to change them.

5. Give gentle prompts, such as "If you notice your mind wandering, gently bring your attention back to your breath."

6. After 3 to 5 minutes, ask the teen(s) to open their eyes and reorient themselves.

DISCUSSION QUESTIONS

▶ What are some sensations you experienced during the activity?

▶ Did you find sitting quietly for a few minutes easy or difficult? Why?

▶ How might becoming more aware of your body sensations help you?

PRO TIPS

▶ Some teen(s) may become uncomfortable sitting quietly for any length of time. Let them know it's okay to open their eyes or take a break.

▶ Remind them that this is a safe place with no judgment.

▶ Reassure them that whatever sensations they are feeling are perfectly fine.

Juggling Thoughts

How mental chatter makes focusing difficult

Level 1
Introduction to Mindfulness

What You'll Need: 4 to 8 balls or other small objects

Duration: 15 minutes

Best for: 3 to 8 people

LEADING THE ACTIVITY

1. Have the group stand in a small circle facing one another.

2. Hand one teen the first object. Ask them to continue passing the object to the person on their right as quickly as possible.

3. Gradually add more objects.

4. After 1 to 2 minutes, pause the activity. Explain that the objects represent mental chatter—the dialogue that goes through our minds on a daily basis.

5. Resume the activity with all available objects for a few minutes and then tell the group to slow down.

6. Explain that mindfulness activities can help slow the mental chatter, making it easier to focus.

7. Allow time for the group to discuss their thoughts.

DISCUSSION QUESTIONS

▶ How did you feel when all the objects were being passed around very quickly?

▶ When does your mental chatter get particularly overwhelming?

▶ What kinds of activities might help slow your mental chatter?

PRO TIPS

▶ Try using objects that represent different concerns (e.g., a book for schoolwork).

▶ If someone gets frustrated during the activity, pause it and allow them all to take a deep breath. Let each teen say what they are feeling at the moment.

▶ If the group needs an extra challenge, ask them to call out common thoughts they have throughout the day while passing around the objects.

Where Do I Feel It?

Noticing how emotions affect the body

What You'll Need: Paper; colored pencils or markers; dry-erase board

Level 1
Introduction to Mindfulness

Duration: 15 to 20 minutes

Best for: 1 to 6 people

LEADING THE ACTIVITY

1. Ask the teen(s) to draw a simple outline of their body.

2. Explain that emotions affect the body in different ways. For example, when someone is angry, they may feel their fists clench or shoulders tense.

3. Have them brainstorm different emotions. Write these on a dry-erase board.

4. Have them pick four emotions and assign a color to each (e.g., yellow for happiness).

5. Give them 5 to 7 minutes to reflect on times they felt these emotions and have them color the affected areas on their body outline.

6. Give them the opportunity to share their drawings and discuss what they noticed.

DISCUSSION QUESTIONS

▶ What areas of your body are most affected by emotions?

▶ What emotions have the biggest effect on your body?

▶ How can being mindful of your body's response to emotions help in everyday life?

PRO TIPS

▶ Instead of reflecting on all the emotions at once, you can break up the period into smaller segments devoted to each emotion.

▶ If they are having a hard time, focus on when they feel the chosen emotions.

▶ Remind the teen(s) there are no right or wrong answers—everyone experiences emotions differently.

What's Going through My Mind?

Using quiet moments to observe passing thoughts

Level 1
Introduction to Mindfulness

What You'll Need: Pens and paper

Duration: 15 minutes

Best for: 1 to 4 people

LEADING THE ACTIVITY

1. Ask the teen(s) to divide a piece of paper into five columns and label them *Planning, Remembering, Emotions, Judgment/Observations,* and *Other.*

2. Explain that sometimes, especially when we're trying to be calm, these types of thoughts can arise and distract us.

3. Discuss the different types of thoughts and have them provide examples.

4. Have them sit quietly for 5 minutes while focusing on their breath. Ask them to quickly check the appropriate column on their paper when they notice a thought, and then let the thought go.

5. Periodically remind them to focus on their breath and notice if they become distracted by thoughts.

6. Allow them to share their findings.

DISCUSSION QUESTIONS

▶ What types of thoughts did you encounter most during this activity?

▶ What thoughts were most distracting or hard to let go?

▶ Would it help to set aside some time each day to notice your thoughts? Why or why not?

PRO TIPS

▶ Choose a calming space that feels safe and distraction-free.

▶ Remind the teen(s) that there are no right or wrong thoughts—the activity is simply a snapshot of what happens to be there.

▶ If they struggle to label their thoughts, let them just jot down the thoughts to discuss later.

What I Like . . . and Don't Like

Observing emotions associated with different situations

Level 1
Introduction to Mindfulness

What You'll Need: Pen and paper

Duration: 10 to 15 minutes

Best for: 1 person

LEADING THE ACTIVITY

1. Ask the teen to divide the paper into four columns and label them *I strongly dislike, I kind of dislike, I kind of like,* and *I really like.*

2. Have them write down one event/scenario for each category.

3. Discuss that we can react emotionally based on particular events. If necessary, help the teen define some emotions.

4. For 2 minutes, have the teen reflect on each event/scenario and write down whatever emotions or thoughts come to mind.

DISCUSSION QUESTIONS

▶ What emotions do you feel most strongly for each scenario?

▶ What emotions did you find most surprising for these scenarios?

▶ How can understanding how you typically react to an event help you in the future?

PRO TIPS

▶ If the teen is having difficulty coming up with emotions for a column, ask them to close their eyes and visualize the event actually happening.

▶ If appropriate, act out an event/scenario to help the teen gain more insight into what emotions may be present.

▶ Use a handout with a list of emotions for teens who find naming emotions challenging.

Tense Up and Release

Using muscle tension and release for relaxation

Level 2
Practicing Mindfulness

What You'll Need: No materials needed

Duration: 10 to 15 minutes

Best for: 1 to 5 people

LEADING THE ACTIVITY

1. Explain that stress and emotions may cause the body to hold tension in different areas. Have the teen(s) give examples of when this can occur.

2. Have them sit or lie down comfortably, then take a couple of deep breaths, closing their eyes if they choose.

3. Explain that when you call out a part of the body, they will tense that part as much as possible for up to 5 seconds. When you say "release," they will release the tension.

4. Guide them through each area of the body.

5. End the exercise by having them tense up their entire body and then release.

6. Give them a few moments to quietly reflect on the experience and the opportunity to discuss.

DISCUSSION QUESTIONS

▶ Which area of your body seemed hardest to relax?

▶ When you're stressed out or overwhelmed, where in the body do you feel most tense?

▶ When would be a good time for you to use this relaxation technique?

PRO TIPS

▶ Make sure the room has minimal distractions.

▶ Be sure to pause for a moment before moving on to the next body part.

▶ If necessary, provide more prompting for better engagement. For example, "Feel your shoulders tense up . . . squeeze . . . squeeze more . . . and now release and feel relaxation flow through the area."

Breathing in Fours

Using mindful breathing to feel grounded and relaxed

Level 2
Practicing Mindfulness

What You'll Need: No materials needed

Duration: 10 to 15 minutes

Best for: 1 to 5 people

LEADING THE ACTIVITY

1. Discuss how mindful breathing can help calm the mind and body during difficult times. Ask the teen(s) when they find it hard to relax.

2. Have them sit comfortably and take a few deep breaths, closing their eyes if they choose.

3. Guide them through a mindful breathing exercise. Have them inhale for 4 counts, hold for 4 counts, exhale for 4 counts, and hold for 4 counts.

4. Continue for 4 to 5 minutes.

5. Give them a few moments to become reoriented.

DISCUSSION QUESTIONS

▶ How did you feel during and after this relaxation technique?

▶ What distractions did you encounter?

▶ Name three real-life scenarios when this technique could be helpful.

PRO TIPS

▶ Let them know it's okay and normal to get distracted during mindfulness exercises. Simply notice the distraction and try to return to the instructions.

▶ For those having difficulty, draw a square on a piece of paper. Ask them to trace one side of the square with their finger for each step in the exercise.

▶ If they have difficulty doing the exercise for an extended period of time, reassure them and ask them to resume their normal breathing and sit quietly as the group finishes.

So Many Distractions!

Reducing distractions to increase concentration

Level 2
Practicing Mindfulness

What You'll Need: Tennis ball and spoon

Duration: 20 minutes

Best for: 4 to 6 people

LEADING THE ACTIVITY

1. Have the group give examples of mental distractions that make it hard to complete a task.

2. Instruct one teen to balance the tennis ball on a spoon while walking across the room.

3. Tell the others to blurt out thoughts that teens deal with every day. For example, "I don't have time to do my homework."

4. Before the teen's next attempt, have them choose an encouraging message for the others to chant. For example, "You've got this."

5. Now have the teen carry the ball across the room with the spoon as the other teens chant the positive message.

6. Repeat the activity with others in the group.

DISCUSSION QUESTIONS

▶ Discuss how the two attempts felt different.

▶ Describe a time when you found it difficult to concentrate because your mind was racing with thoughts.

▶ What are some advantages of learning to calm your thoughts using mindfulness?

PRO TIPS

▶ Brainstorm thoughts to blurt out before starting the activity to ensure that what the teens come up with is appropriate and respectful.

▶ If the activity feels too easy, add obstacles, like walking around chairs.

▶ If the activity is too hard, modify it by having teens carry the tennis ball in the palms of their hands.

Cultivating Gratitude

Appreciating the positives
in different aspects of life

Level 2
Practicing Mindfulness

What You'll Need: Paper; colored pencils or markers

Duration: 15 to 20 minutes

Best for: 2 or 3 people

LEADING THE ACTIVITY

1. Ask the teens to define gratitude and provide examples.

2. Instruct them to draw a tree with at least five large branches.

3. On each branch, have them write down one major aspect of their life—school, family, friends, etc.

4. Explain how developing a sense of gratitude can improve your mood and lead to greater appreciation for life.

5. Have them draw four leaves on each branch and fill them with single words or short phrases describing why they are grateful about this aspect of their life.

6. Encourage them to share their drawings.

DISCUSSION QUESTIONS

▶ Which leaves were the easiest to fill in?

▶ Were there any areas of your life that you had a hard time feeling grateful about?

▶ How has this activity changed the way you view the circumstances in your life?

PRO TIPS

▶ Brainstorm examples of gratitude for teens having a difficult time filling in the leaves.

▶ Challenge teens to add more leaves to each branch as they reflect.

▶ Encourage them to hang their gratitude tree somewhere they can see it every day.

One Mindful Step at a Time

Experiencing mindfulness using a commonplace activity

Level 2
Practicing Mindfulness

What You'll Need: Masking tape

Duration: 10 to 15 minutes

Best for: 1 to 5 people

Prep: Create a walking path around the room using masking tape.

LEADING THE ACTIVITY

1. Discuss mindfulness and how even simple activities like walking can be an opportunity to practice it.

2. Have teen(s) line up at one point on the path.

3. Instruct them to walk around the path, focusing their attention on each step they take. They can count each step, mentally say, "right foot, left foot," or focus on how each foot feels as it makes contact with the floor.

4. Allow teen(s) to walk the path for 4 to 7 minutes. Gently remind them to return their focus to their steps if they notice their mind wandering.

5. Give teen(s) a chance to reflect on the experience.

DISCUSSION QUESTIONS

▶ How did you feel while attempting mindful walking?

▶ How often did you have to return your focus to the act of walking?

▶ What are some other simple activities that can help you practice mindfulness?

PRO TIPS

▶ Adjust the duration of the activity based on how your group is responding.

▶ If a larger area is available (even outside), use it instead.

▶ Remind teen(s) that distracting thoughts are normal. If they notice that they are distracted, they can pause for a moment, take a few deep breaths, and then return to the activity.

Clouds in the Sky

Becoming less reactive
in difficult moments

Level 3
Incorporating Mindfulness
into Daily Life

What You'll Need: No materials needed

Duration: 15 minutes

Best for: 1 to 5 people

Prep: Create a space where teens can sit comfortably
with minimal distractions.

LEADING THE ACTIVITY

1. Explain how being aware of thoughts, feelings, and emotions as they occur can prevent behaviors we may regret.

2. Have the teen(s) take a few deep breaths, settle in, and picture a deep blue sky while trying to clear their mind.

3. Tell them to imagine any thought, feeling, or emotion that arises as just a cloud floating by. When it passes, they can return their focus to the blue sky.

4. Remind them that the clouds are not them, just something passing through them. They are the blue sky.

5. Continue the exercise for 5 to 7 minutes, gently reminding them about the clouds.

6. Allow teen(s) to reorient to the room and start discussion.

DISCUSSION QUESTIONS

▶ How often did you encounter clouds passing through your sky?

▶ What difficulties did you have allowing thoughts or emotions to pass?

▶ How does realizing that your thoughts and emotions are just temporary clouds change your perspective?

PRO TIPS

▶ Limit any unnecessary distractions during the exercise.

▶ If anyone becomes uncomfortable, let them stop the exercise and sit quietly.

▶ Gradually increase the duration of the meditation if you are repeating it with the same teen or group.

Take a Step Back

Responding more calmly
to difficult people

Level 3
Incorporating Mindfulness
into Daily Life

What You'll Need: No materials needed

Duration: 15 to 20 minutes

Best for: 2 to 6 people

LEADING THE ACTIVITY

1. Discuss how mindful "time-outs" can help when dealing with a difficult person.

2. Brainstorm scenarios in which someone might make the teens angry or upset.

3. Choose one scenario.

4. Ask one teen to be the difficult person and another to be someone trying to respond calmly.

5. Have them act out the scenario for about a minute.

6. Stop the acting by saying, "Breathe and take a step back."

7. Have the person trying to react calmly state how they are feeling by using an "I" statement (e.g., "I am frustrated because . . ").

8. Troubleshoot ways to effectively deal with this scenario.

9. Repeat this activity using different scenarios.

10. Discuss how taking a few mindful moments allows a person to react calmly.

DISCUSSION QUESTIONS

▶ Describe a time when a difficult person got the better of you.

▶ What are some ways you can take a quick "time-out" during difficult situations?

▶ What are some triggers that cause you to feel angry or upset?

PRO TIPS

▶ Make sure the teens remain respectful while interacting.

▶ Closely monitor the scenarios and quickly pause the activity before a teen becomes visibly upset.

▶ If any teen has a history of trauma, be careful in selecting scenarios that may retraumatize.

A Mind Map of My Day

Understanding our
daily positive and
negative thoughts

Level 3
Incorporating Mindfulness
into Daily Life

What You'll Need: Pencils and paper

Duration: 15 to 20 minutes

Best for: 1 to 6 people

LEADING THE ACTIVITY

1. Have the teen(s) spend a minute or two quietly reflecting on the past couple of days.

2. On different parts of a piece of paper, have them write down some places where they spent time over the last few days.

3. Ask them to circle each place and draw lines branching out from it.

4. At the end of each line, have them write thoughts and emotions associated with the place.

5. Next to each thought, ask them to put a "+" or "–" to indicate a positive or negative thought.

6. Allow them to share, as they feel comfortable, about the mind map and discuss.

DISCUSSION QUESTIONS

▶ What surprised you about your mind map?

▶ Did you notice any recurring themes in your thoughts or emotions about each place?

▶ How might you cope better with difficult places if you have a better understanding of how they affect you?

PRO TIPS

▶ Provide an example of a mind map to give teen(s) a better idea of the activity.

▶ If time permits, allow quiet reflection (2 to 3 minutes) for each place they listed on the mind map.

▶ Reassure teen(s) that they have complete control over what they want to share.

Calm Bottles

Encouraging mindfulness
through crafts

Level 3
Incorporating Mindfulness
into Daily Life

What You'll Need: Jars or water bottles; warm tap water;
at least three colors of glitter; school glue; funnels;
food coloring; markers

Duration: 15 to 20 minutes

Best for: 1 to 5 people

LEADING THE ACTIVITY

1. Instruct the teen(s) to:
   - Fill a bottle a third of the way with glue.
   - Using a funnel, add half a teaspoon each of (at least) three colors of glitter.
   - Fill the bottle nearly to the top with warm water, cap it, and shake.
   - If the glitter falls too fast, add more glue. If not, add more water.
   - If desired, add a couple drops of food coloring.
   - Seal the cap with glue.
2. Discuss how the glitter can represent thoughts and feelings. When you're in a difficult situation, you may feel "shaken up," making it hard to see through the mix of thoughts, feelings, and emotions.
3. Ask the teen(s) to write a calming message on their bottles, such as "I'm in control."
4. Have them think of a recent problem they experienced, and then shake their bottles.
5. Have them take deep breaths and calmly watch the glitter settle.

DISCUSSION QUESTIONS

▶ Describe a time when you felt overwhelmed by a troubling situation.

▶ What are some thoughts, feelings, and urges that sometimes make it difficult to think clearly?

▶ How can using your calm bottle help you return to the present moment?

PRO TIPS

▶ Use better quality water bottles to make the craft more durable.

▶ Glycerin or dish soap can replace glue to slow down the glitter.

▶ Encourage teen(s) to use the calm bottle if they have trouble focusing on other mindfulness activities.

Lovingkindness Meditation

Projecting compassion and goodwill to loved ones—and difficult people

Level 3
Incorporating Mindfulness into Daily Life

What You'll Need: No materials needed

Duration: 15 minutes

Best for: 1 to 5 people

LEADING THE ACTIVITY

1. Define compassion and discuss how feeling compassion toward others can help you see people in a different way.

2. Ask teen(s) to sit or lie down in a comfortable position and take a few deep breaths.

3. Guide them using the following steps:

   - Imagine yourself in a place where you are comfortable and happy. Mentally say to yourself, "May I be happy, may I be well, may I be free from pain."

   - Picture someone you love walking into this place. Imagine you are projecting waves of love to this other person. In your mind, tell this person, "May you be happy, may you be well, may you be free from pain." Picture this person receiving your goodwill and imagine their response.

   - Picture someone you feel neutral about. Repeat the actions in the previous step.

   - Picture someone you find difficult. Repeat the process.

4. Take a few minutes to allow them to reorient before discussing.

DISCUSSION QUESTIONS

► How do you feel after doing this meditation?

► How does imagining influencing someone in a positive way affect how you view that person?

PRO TIPS

► During the meditation, give prompts to help teens visualize the experience. For example, "What does the room look like?"

► Remind teen(s) that whatever they picture or feel is perfectly right for the present moment.

CHAPTER 2

SELF-ESTEEM

Self-esteem is a person's overall sense of self-worth—how the individual appreciates and feels about self. Teens struggle with self-esteem on an almost daily basis due to pressures from family, peers, and even the mirror. Negative events during these formative years can put a major dent in a teen's self-esteem.

Helping a teen cultivate self-esteem can have lasting positive effects. Teens with good self-esteem are more confident and resilient and less likely to engage in damaging behaviors like substance abuse.

The activities in this chapter are divided into three levels. Understanding Self-Esteem (Level 1) helps teens get a better understanding of how they feel about themselves. What's Affecting Self-Esteem? (Level 2) helps teens understand what's contributing to negative or positive self-esteem. Building Self-Esteem (Level 3) helps build self-esteem and foster a growth mindset.

What I Like About Myself

Taking a closer look at teens' positive qualities

Level 1
Understanding
Self-Esteem

What You'll Need: Paper; pens; markers or colored pencils

Duration: 20 minutes

Best for: 2 to 6 people

LEADING THE ACTIVITY

1. Discuss how focusing on our positive qualities can help improve self-esteem.

2. Have the group give examples of positive qualities.

3. Give them a few minutes to quietly brainstorm their own personal positive qualities and write them on a piece of paper.

4. Have them rank their favorite qualities from 1 to 10.

5. Give them about 10 minutes to either write a "viral video" script or make a small poster of their positive qualities.

6. Have each teen present their positive qualities to the group.

7. Discuss the presentations.

DISCUSSION QUESTIONS

▶ What positive qualities were most common?

▶ What positive qualities did you find surprising or interesting?

▶ How can focusing on all the good you have to offer help you during difficult times?

PRO TIPS

▶ As teens brainstorm their positive traits, give prompts to help spark ideas. For example, "What ways do you make your family proud?"

▶ Shy teens may have trouble talking about themselves. Encourage them to create the poster and present it anyway—and to ask for help from a more outgoing teen.

▶ If necessary, change the suggested number of positive qualities for teens to rank.

Identifying Self-Talk

Looking at the positive
and negative messages
we tell ourselves

Level 1
Understanding
Self-Esteem

What You'll Need: Pencils; small strips of paper
(10 per person); three buckets or wastebaskets

Duration: 10 to 15 minutes

Best for: 1 to 5 people

LEADING THE ACTIVITY

1. Define **self-talk** as internal dialogue that can be both positive and negative. Discuss how it can affect our mood and self-esteem. Allow the teen(s) to share examples.

2. Give them 10 strips of paper and a pencil. On each strip, have them write examples of self-talk they experience or they think others experience.

3. While they are writing, label the buckets or wastebaskets *Positive, Negative,* and *Neutral,* and place them a few feet away from the teen(s).

4. Once they have finished writing, have them share what they wrote, then crumple up the paper, and toss it into one of the three buckets.

5. Continue until all strips of paper are used.

DISCUSSION QUESTIONS

▶ What was the most common type of self-talk you identified? Why do you think so?

▶ What self-talk did you experience while doing this activity?

▶ How can becoming more aware of your self-talk help improve how you feel each day?

PRO TIPS

▶ Make it fun! Turn throwing the pieces of paper into the buckets into a game.

▶ If someone misses a bucket, have them read another similar thought before getting another chance to toss it into the bucket.

▶ To help generate more ideas, give examples of situations where teens may experience self-talk.

I Made It This Far

Helping teens celebrate
their successes

Level 1
Understanding
Self-Esteem

What You'll Need: Masking tape; small prize(s) or certificate(s)
of completion

Duration: 10 to 15 minutes

Best for: 1 to 5 people

Prep: Place five to seven strips of masking tape on the floor
to represent hurdles.

LEADING THE ACTIVITY

1. Discuss how celebrating recent successes or "wins" can help shift a negative
    perspective to a positive one. Have teen(s) provide examples of "wins."

2. Explain that each piece of tape represents a challenge or hurdle they faced
    throughout their daily life. To "jump" over the hurdle, they must share a recent
    win they experienced.

3. At each piece of tape, have teen(s) discuss a challenge they faced. They can step
    over the piece of tape once they have talked about how they overcame the chal-
    lenge for a "win."

4. After they step over all of the hurdles, give them a small prize or certificate
    of completion honoring them for celebrating positive successes.

DISCUSSION QUESTIONS

▸ How do you feel after taking a closer look at your recent wins?

▸ What recent success makes you the proudest?

▸ What are some simple things you can do to celebrate jumping over life's hurdles?

PRO TIPS

▸ Remind teen(s) that success comes in all sizes. Every win is a jump over a hurdle.

▸ If time allows, have them give an example of when they fell short of a personal
"win" and suggest a way to approach the situation differently.

▸ Everyone experiences successes differently—be sure to intervene if someone
belittles another person's win.

Famous Imperfections

Realizing that even the most revered people aren't perfect

Understanding
Self-Esteem

What You'll Need: Dry-erase board and markers

Duration: 20 minutes

Best for: 2 to 6 people

LEADING THE ACTIVITY

1. Have teens provide a definition of **perfectionism,** a personality trait characterized by the need to be perfect. Discuss whether being perfect is even possible.

2. Have them name five to eight famous people some may consider perfect. Write their names on a dry-erase board.

3. Give teens a couple of minutes to discuss what they've heard about each celebrity. Encourage a spirited, respectful debate on how they view each celebrity.

4. After 2 to 4 minutes, have them list some imperfections each celebrity may have.

5. Continue this process with each name on the board.

6. Discuss how everyone has imperfections and how accepting and even embracing them can improve self-esteem.

DISCUSSION QUESTIONS

▶ Do you feel perfection is attainable? Why or why not?

▶ After considering the imperfections of celebrities, how can you become more accepting of yourself?

▶ How can perfectionism affect your self-esteem?

PRO TIPS

▶ You can substitute superheroes, literary characters, or any other person who resonates with the teens you work with.

▶ Keep the debate respectful. Some teens have strong emotional ties to certain celebrities and may get upset if they feel the person is being attacked.

▶ Remind teens that some celebrity gossip is just gossip; make it a quick teachable moment about how gossip can be toxic for both celebrities and everyday people.

What's Important to Me

Creating a collage
of personal values

Level 1
Understanding
Self-Esteem

What You'll Need: Poster board or large pieces of paper; magazines or other items with images or words that can be clipped; scissors; glue; colored pencils and markers; access to computer and printer (optional)

Duration: 20 minutes

Best for: 1 to 6 people

LEADING THE ACTIVITY

1. Have the teen(s) define the meaning of values and provide relevant examples.

2. Discuss how sticking to or ignoring personal values can affect self-esteem.

3. With the materials provided, allow them to create a collage representing the values most important to them. They can clip pictures or words, draw pictures, write words, or use any other form of creative expression.

4. Give teen(s) a chance to present their collage to the group.

DISCUSSION QUESTIONS

▶ What values are most important to you? Why?

▶ What common values have you noticed in the group? Different values?

▶ Describe a time when your personal values were challenged and how you reacted.

PRO TIPS

▶ Remind the teen(s) that values are highly personal and there are no right or wrong answers.

▶ If time and resources allow, give teens a chance to print some pictures from the internet—especially if you don't have access to magazines.

▶ If you are lacking resources, teen(s) can do this activity by drawing a personal advertisement about their values.

What Am I Telling Myself?

Identifying self-talk habits
with the help of peers

Level 2
What's Affecting
Self-Esteem?

What You'll Need: Pencils; sticky notes; dry-erase board
and markers

Duration: 20 minutes

Best for: 2 to 6 people

Prep: Create a list of open-ended "I" statements the teens
can easily finish (e.g., "So far my day has been . . . " or
"In five years I will . . . ").

LEADING THE ACTIVITY

1. Define self-talk and discuss ways it can be positive or negative.

2. Read an open-ended statement and have the teens write their responses on
    sticky notes.

3. Collect and shuffle the responses.

4. Read each response out loud and have them determine if it's positive or negative
    self-talk. Stick each response on the dry-erase board, divided into positive or
    negative self-talk.

5. Repeat this process with the rest of the statements.

DISCUSSION QUESTIONS

▶ Did some statements generate more positive self-talk? Negative self-talk?
Why do you think this happened?

▶ Can you take a negative self-talk example and turn it into a positive one?

▶ How can becoming more aware of your self-talk help build self-esteem?

PRO TIPS

▶ If time allows, have teens suggest open-ended statements to use in the activity.

▶ Although responses will be anonymous, teens can be sensitive if their responses
are judged harshly. Encourage the group to give their opinions respectfully.

▶ Remind teens that there are no right or wrong answers to the statements.

What Is Social Media Telling Me?

Exploring social media
and teens' self-esteem

Level 2
What's Affecting
Self-Esteem?

What You'll Need: Dry-erase board and markers; pencils; paper

Duration: 15 to 20 minutes

Best for: 2 to 8 people

LEADING THE ACTIVITY

1. Have the teens call out their favorite social media outlets and list them on the dry-erase board. Discuss how often they engage with social media.

2. Talk about how some social media posts can create unrealistic expectations (misleading posts, photo filters, etc.).

3. On a piece of paper, have them create what they perceive to be an unrealistic social media post.

4. Allow them to share examples and discuss why they are unrealistic.

5. Discuss how unrealistic posts can affect self-esteem.

DISCUSSION QUESTIONS

▶ Has social media ever affected your self-esteem? Why or why not?

▶ Have you ever posted unrealistic things on social media? What motivated you?

▶ How can the ability to identify unrealistic posts make you more resistant to the influence of social media?

PRO TIPS

▶ Since social media is an important aspect of many teens' lives, be sure to also highlight the positive aspects of connecting socially online.

▶ Give teens a chance to brainstorm what a more realistic post would look like.

▶ Don't provide all of the answers. Let the teens come up with different interpretations to counter unrealistic expectations.

Friendship Deal Breakers

Identifying qualities that make it hard to maintain a friendship

Level 2
What's Affecting Self-Esteem?

What You'll Need: Pencils and paper

Duration: 15 to 20 minutes

Best for: 2 to 6 people

LEADING THE ACTIVITY

1. Have the teens discuss what qualities they look for in good friendships and relationships. Talk about why these qualities are important.

2. Discuss qualities that can put a strain on friendships. Have them brainstorm some deal breakers that would force them to say "no" to a friendship or relationship (e.g., big ego, gets in trouble often).

3. Talk about healthy boundaries and why it is important to create distance from people who possess these deal breakers.

4. Role-play ways they can say "no" to other teens with these deal-breaker characteristics.

DISCUSSION QUESTIONS

▶ Why did you select these particular deal breakers?

▶ Describe a time when you had a hard time saying "no" to a friend.

▶ How can creating healthy boundaries help your self-esteem?

PRO TIPS

▶ Take time to discuss each deal breaker and how it can create a negative or destructive friendship.

▶ If a teen is having trouble with role-playing, allow them to "tap out" and ask another person in the group to complete the role-play.

▶ Give teens a chance to share stories of the negative consequences from past friendships or relationships.

Being Kind to My Body

Using creative expression to appreciate the body

Level 2
What's Affecting
Self-Esteem?

What You'll Need: Pencils and paper; markers; colored pencils; watercolor paints; brushes, or any other available art supplies

Duration: 15 to 20 minutes

Best for: 2 to 6 people

LEADING THE ACTIVITY

1. Talk about how being kind to and accepting of oneself can improve self-esteem.

2. In the middle of a piece of paper, have the teens write a haiku that positively highlights their own physical attributes. (A **haiku** is a simple three-line poem in which the first line has five syllables, the second line has seven syllables, and the third line has five syllables.)

3. Ask them to decorate their poems with any available art supplies.

4. Have them present the art project to the group and ask the group to respond with only positive feedback.

DISCUSSION QUESTIONS

▶ What were some of the positive qualities you considered while writing the haiku?

▶ What were some of the surprising or recurring themes you noticed from others in the group?

▶ How do you feel about sharing your positive qualities with the group?

PRO TIPS

▶ Provide examples of haikus to help teens complete the project.

▶ If a teen is struggling with the haiku, start with a prompt or help them with the first line.

▶ If possible, have them hang up the haikus where they can be viewed and appreciated by others.

Growing from Mistakes

Discovering how mistakes
can be a learning
opportunity

Level 2
What's Affecting
Self-Esteem

What You'll Need: Pencils and paper; colored pencils
and/or markers

Duration: 15 to 20 minutes

Best for: 2 to 6 people

LEADING THE ACTIVITY

1. Discuss how mistakes sometimes affect how we feel about ourselves.

2. Give the teens the following instructions:

   - Draw the trunk of a tree on a piece of paper. At the base of the trunk, write down a mistake that affected your life.

   - A bit higher on the trunk, jot down what it felt like to make that mistake.

   - Now, draw four main branches of the tree. Along each branch, write down the specific area of your life that was affected by the mistake.

   - At the end of the branches, draw some leaves and fill them with any lessons you learned from your mistake in that specific area of your life.

   - Finally, draw a sun above the tree. Inside the sun, write down the most important learning opportunity you gained from the mistake.

3. Allow the teens to decorate the drawing in any way they choose.

4. Share and discuss the artwork.

DISCUSSION QUESTIONS

▶ What made you choose this particular mistake?

▶ Was it easy to recover from this mistake? Why or why not?

▶ How can analyzing and learning from your mistakes help build your self-esteem?

PRO TIPS

▶ If a teen is having trouble with the activity, have them talk through their situation with the others.

▶ Discuss how a tree endures many changes throughout its lifetime. Compare a mistake to a dry season or lightning strike that the tree overcomes.

My Dream Vacation

Practicing self-care and
boosting self-esteem

What You'll Need: Pencils; paper; magazines; images
from the internet (if possible); colored pencils; markers

Level 3
Building Self-Esteem

Duration: 20 minutes

Best for: 1 to 5 people

LEADING THE ACTIVITY

1. Discuss how being kind to yourself can help improve your mood and enhance self-esteem. Have the teen(s) give a few quick examples of ways to be kind to themselves.

2. Ask them to imagine a dream vacation where they get whatever they need to pamper and be kind to themselves.

3. Have them take 10 minutes to create an advertisement for their self-care dream vacation, using the listed supplies.

4. Allow them to share their ads and why they chose certain experiences.

DISCUSSION QUESTIONS

▶ What do you like best about your dream vacation? Why?

▶ What self-care aspects of your dream vacation can you practice today?

▶ How can taking a little time each day/week to be kind to yourself help you feel better physically, mentally, and emotionally?

PRO TIPS

▶ Encourage teen(s) to be as creative as possible. The goal of their ad is to persuade others that being kind to ourselves is important.

▶ If you are familiar with your teen(s) already, try to supply images you feel will resonate with them.

▶ If the teen(s) are more outgoing, allow them to present their ad as a television or internet commercial.

Nothing Compares to Me

Developing a greater appreciation of our bodies

Level 3
Building Self-Esteem

What You'll Need: Pencils and paper

Duration: 15 to 20 minutes

Best for: 1 to 6 people

LEADING THE ACTIVITY

1. Discuss how we often take our bodies for granted.

2. Explain that this exercise is an opportunity to celebrate and give gratitude to our bodies.

3. Allow the teen(s) to settle in a comfortable position and take a few deep breaths.

4. Talk about some of the body's basic functions, like breathing and digestion.

5. Discuss how the body helps us perform different physical activities.

6. Guide the teen(s) to discuss the remarkable traits their own bodies possess— physical, creative, and intellectual. Which of their body's abilities sets them apart from others?

7. Allow them a minute to reflect on their thoughts.

8. Have them list five ways they feel grateful for their bodies and discuss.

DISCUSSION QUESTIONS

▶ Name three things about your body you often take for granted.

▶ In what ways has this activity given you a better appreciation of your body?

▶ How can regularly giving gratitude to your body help your self-esteem and personal behaviors?

PRO TIPS

▶ Make the guided discussion as individualized as possible, depending on how well you know your teen(s).

▶ Provide short pauses during the guided portion to allow teens to process and reflect.

▶ When discussing body functions, be mindful of the physical capabilities of your teen(s), especially those with disabilities.

My Small Book of Big Goals

Developing a growth
mindset by setting goals

What You'll Need: Pencils; small notebooks or notepads

Duration: 20 to 25 minutes

Level 3
Building Self-Esteem

Best for: 1 to 6 people

LEADING THE ACTIVITY

1. Talk about how to use goals and how they can help different aspects of life.

2. Discuss the difference between short-term goals and long-term goals.

3. In a small notebook, have teen(s) write down what they want to improve about their lives and then privately brainstorm goals they could set to help them make these improvements.

4. Allow them to share their goals, if they wish. Discuss the goals and how some might be improved.

5. Have them choose one of the improvements they listed in their notebook and write down a short-term, medium-term, and long-term goal for accomplishing it.

6. Have them write a quick progress note toward these goals each day.

DISCUSSION QUESTIONS

▶ Have you ever tried setting goals for yourself before? What were the results?

▶ Do you feel the goals you created today are reasonable and attainable? Why or why not?

▶ How can goal-setting help improve self-esteem?

PRO TIPS

▶ If teen(s) are having a difficult time coming up with reasonable, measurable goals, talk them through some examples.

▶ This activity is more effective if you have weekly or periodic check-ins with the teen(s).

▶ Explain that it's okay if they don't reach their goal. Some goals need modifications to be more realistic.

Popular Values

Identifying personal values and discovering what values teens have in common

Level 3
Building Self-Esteem

What You'll Need: Pencils and paper; dry-erase board and marker

Duration: 20 to 25 minutes

Best for: 2 to 8 people

LEADING THE ACTIVITY

1. Define **personal values** and provide examples such as fearlessness and honesty.

2. Brainstorm some values and discuss what each looks like.

3. Talk about why knowing and honoring your values can help maintain and/or improve self-esteem.

4. Have each teen list their top five values on a sheet of paper.

5. Collect the papers and determine the five most popular values for the group.

6. Write numbers 1 through 5 on a dry-erase board.

7. Ask teens to guess the top answers and write the correct ones on the board.

8. Discuss what made these values so important to them.

DISCUSSION QUESTIONS

▶ What values did you think would be the most popular?

▶ Which results surprised you?

▶ How can you stick to your values every day? How can that help your self-esteem?

PRO TIPS

▶ Reveal answers in any way that works best. You could give each teen chances to guess or make it like a game show.

▶ Provide a list of values to the teens to expand their knowledge.

▶ Conduct a short icebreaker activity while you are tabulating the answers, especially if you have a larger group.

Affirmation Cards

Using positive affirmations to bounce back from failures and develop a growth mindset

Level 3
Building Self-Esteem

What You'll Need: Note cards (or any type of paper); pencils; colored pencils; markers

Duration: 15 to 20 minutes

Best for: 1 to 8 people

LEADING THE ACTIVITY

1. Discuss how using **positive affirmations**, or simple empowering phrases, can change negative self-talk, help you grow, and move on after difficult times.

2. Give examples starting with "I am . . ." that address past mistakes or trigger positive thoughts to create a growth mindset. For example, "I am strong."

3. Have the teen(s) reflect on an aspect of life or thought patterns they would like to change.

4. Guide them to create a positive affirmation—for example, "I accept myself as I am."

5. Have them write the affirmation on a note card, decorate it if they wish, and put it in an easily accessible place to use in a troubling moment.

6. Remind them to use it as often as possible—even while doing mundane tasks.

7. Encourage them to note in a daily journal when they've used the affirmation and how it increased their self-esteem and changed negative thoughts.

DISCUSSION QUESTIONS

▶ What made you choose your affirmation?

▶ When do you plan to use your positive affirmation?

▶ How do you think positive affirmations can help you build self-esteem and a more positive future?

PRO TIPS

▶ Provide a variety of positive affirmations to inspire the teen(s) to find one that really resonates.

▶ Give examples of when positive affirmations can be especially helpful—for example, when feeling inadequate around others.

CHAPTER 3

COMMUNICATION SKILLS

Communication skills are the tools we use to relate to one another. Experiential activities are a great way to engage teens while they learn, practice, and develop communication skills.

We all know communication is essential to maintain professional and personal relationships. Teens are just beginning to build this skill. Learning effective and appropriate communication early on can help a teen grow into a more assertive, self-assured, and self-aware person.

The activities in this chapter are divided into three levels: Communication Basics (Level 1), Types of Communication (Level 2), and Communication in Everyday Life (Level 3). Use Level 1 activities to work on developing essential communication skills. Level 2 activities help teens take a closer look at the intricacies of communication. Level 3 helps teens practice applying their communication skills in common situations.

Active Listening

Using active listening to learn more about others

Level 1
Communication Basics

What You'll Need: No materials needed

Duration: 15 to 20 minutes

Best for: 2 to 10 people

LEADING THE ACTIVITY

1. Define **active listening** as a listening technique that focuses on observing and remembering what the other person is saying to better understand their message. Give examples of active listening skills, such as eye contact and paraphrasing.

2. Ask the teens to demonstrate active and/or poor listening skills.

3. Pair up teens and instruct one teen to introduce themself while the other uses active listening. Give the teens introducing themselves 3 minutes to speak.

4. After the 3 minutes, have the active listening teens introduce their partners to the others.

5. Have them switch roles and repeat the activity.

6. Discuss how active listening helped them learn more about their partner.

DISCUSSION QUESTIONS

▶ What active listening skills did you find challenging? Easy?

▶ How did it feel when your partner was using active listening while you introduced yourself?

▶ How can active listening help you become a better communicator?

PRO TIPS

▶ If possible, pair teens up with someone they don't know very well.

▶ Provide a list of things the teens could mention about themselves to encourage more conversation.

▶ After the activity, mention some of the positive examples of active listening you noticed.

Guess My Emotion

Acting out emotions using nonverbal communication

Level 1
Communication Basics

What You'll Need: No materials needed

Duration: 15 to 20 minutes

Best for: 2 to 10 people

LEADING THE ACTIVITY

1. Define **nonverbal communication** and note that it's just as important as the words we use.

2. Give examples of nonverbal communication, such as balled-up fists expressing frustration or crossed arms signaling that someone isn't listening.

3. Have one teen act out an emotion without using words or sounds. Have the others guess the emotion.

4. Give each teen a couple of opportunities to act out different emotions.

5. Discuss how understanding and identifying nonverbal communication can help teens be more empathetic and "tuned-in" during interactions.

DISCUSSION QUESTIONS

▶ Describe a time when you noticed how someone was feeling before they said anything. What did you see?

▶ Can you think of a time when your nonverbal communication sent contradictory messages?

▶ How can being more mindful of nonverbal communication allow you to relate better to others?

PRO TIPS

▶ Instead of letting the teens choose the emotions they act out, provide a list of emotions and assign them to the teens.

▶ Have teens pair up to act out certain emotions.

▶ When a teen guesses the correct emotion, ask what nonverbal cues gave it away.

Keep the Candy!

Using assertive communication to achieve a goal

Level 1
Communication Basics

What You'll Need: Candy or any other desirable items (about five pieces for each teen)

Duration: 15 to 20 minutes

Best for: 2 to 8 people

LEADING THE ACTIVITY

1. Define and give examples of **assertive communication,** using the three c's: confidence, clarity, and control.

2. Have the teens brainstorm examples of assertive communication and then discuss each example: Are they truly assertive or actually passive or aggressive?

3. Give one teen several pieces of candy. Give each of the other teens 1 to 2 minutes to try to persuade the teen to give them the candy. Tell the teen with the candy to use assertive communication to keep it.

4. When time is up, have the teens summarize the experience.

5. Give each of the other teens a turn to hold the candy and use assertive communication to keep it.

6. Discuss the different methods of communication used throughout the activity.

DISCUSSION QUESTIONS

▶ How did you feel while others were trying to get the candy from you? How were you assertive?

▶ Talk about a time when using assertive communication would have been more effective than being aggressive or passive.

▶ What are the advantages of mastering assertive communication?

PRO TIPS

▶ If a teen is becoming upset or aggressive during the activity, do a quick "time-out and check-in" session to reorient the group.

▶ After each 1- to 2-minute session, highlight one great quote or behavior you noticed that demonstrated appropriate assertive communication.

Apologizing Sincerely

Encouraging teens to apologize appropriately and respectfully

Level 1
Communication Basics

What You'll Need: Plastic Easter eggs filled with coins (or another object for teens to toss to each other)

Duration: 10 to 15 minutes

Best for: 4 to 14 people

LEADING THE ACTIVITY

1. Talk about right and wrong ways to apologize. Highlight good examples such as being sincere and not making excuses.

2. Have teens pair up and form two lines, facing each other about three feet apart.

3. Hand out the eggs. Then have each pair take turns throwing their egg back and forth. Each time an egg is caught, teens take a step backward.

4. When someone misses or drops an egg, ask them to sincerely apologize.

5. If you determine that they gave a sincere apology, allow the game to continue.

6. If you can't determine which teen of the pair is at fault, have both apologize.

7. If you determine an apology isn't sincere, have the pair step away and discuss.

8. End the game when there is only one pair left or the pairs are 10 feet apart.

9. Have the teens who were asked to leave the game discuss why their apologies weren't sincere and how they could be improved.

DISCUSSION QUESTIONS

▶ Describe how it felt to apologize to your teammate during the game.

▶ When someone apologized to you, what made you feel it was sincere?

▶ How can apologizing sincerely be an important communication skill?

PRO TIPS

▶ Instead of allowing a pair to continue after every sincere apology, you can limit the number of apologies players can make to remain in the game.

▶ If you're playing in a smaller area, add challenges with each throw. For example, ask both teens to stand on one foot.

Can You Please Clarify?

Asking clarifying questions to understand what others are saying

Level 1
Communication Basics

What You'll Need: No materials needed

Duration: 20 to 25 minutes

Best for: 2 to 10 people

LEADING THE ACTIVITY

1. Define **clarifying questions** and discuss how they can be helpful to better understand what someone is saying.

2. Discuss the characteristics of clarifying questions: they're specific, they summarize what the other person said, and they're honest about not understanding without placing blame.

3. Have teens pair up. Instruct one teen to discuss a personal interest the other teen may not know much about, such as their favorite musician. Encourage the other teen to ask clarifying questions. Allow 3 to 4 minutes for them to talk.

4. After the conversation, have the listening teens discuss how their clarifying questions helped them better understand what the speaker was saying.

5. Switch roles and repeat.

DISCUSSION QUESTIONS

▶ How did clarifying questions help you better understand the conversation? What clarifying questions worked best for you?

▶ How did you feel while being asked clarifying questions?

▶ Name some times when clarifying questions can be especially helpful.

PRO TIPS

▶ If this concept is new to the group, allow two teens to participate in the activity while the rest of the group watches. Discuss the interactions afterward.

▶ To make this a one-on-one activity, talk about a topic that the teen can ask clarifying questions about.

▶ Provide a list of examples of clarifying questions to help teens struggling with the concept.

Address Your Audience

Examining how teens communicate differently with different audiences

Level 2
Types of Communication

What You'll Need: Paper; pencils; colored pencils

Duration: 20 to 25 minutes

Best for: 1 to 6 people

LEADING THE ACTIVITY

1. Describe how we communicate differently with different types of people—friends, parents, teachers, bosses, etc.

2. Discuss why we communicate differently depending on the audience.

3. Have the teen(s) act out a couple of scenarios illustrating how they speak to different types of people.

4. Ask them to create a few comics strips showing how they communicate in different scenarios.

5. Have them present their comic strips and discuss.

DISCUSSION QUESTIONS

▶ What are some key differences in the way you talk to different groups of people?

▶ What groups of people do you have the most trouble communicating with, and why?

▶ Why is it important to understand the audience when communicating?

PRO TIPS

▶ If time allows, have the teen(s) act out inappropriate communicating (for example, talking to their boss as if they were a friend).

▶ If necessary, provide example scenarios and prompts for their comic strips.

▶ Depending on the group and amount of time you have, you can omit the comic strips and perform more role-plays.

Passive, Assertive, or Aggressive?

Understanding the differences between passive, aggressive, and assertive communication

Level 2
Types of Communication

What You'll Need: Paper; hole puncher; long section of thick string; duct or other strong tape

Duration: 15 to 20 minutes

Best for: 3 to 6 people

Prep: Punch a hole near the edge on small sheets of paper (at least three per person in the group) and thread a piece of string through it.

LEADING THE ACTIVITY

1. Define and provide examples of passive, aggressive, and assertive communication.

2. Provide teens with small blank sheets of paper and have them write their own examples of these types of communication.

3. Hang up and secure the string where teens can reach it.

4. Have each teen pull a piece of paper off the string and read the phrase out loud. Ask that teen to guess which type of communication the phrase illustrates and allow the group to give feedback.

5. Continue until all of the pieces of paper are used.

DISCUSSION QUESTIONS

▶ What phrases were hard to interpret? Why?

▶ What type of communication do you notice yourself using most often?

▶ How can understanding effective ways to be assertive help you get your point across?

PRO TIPS

▶ If you don't have a string, put the pieces of paper facedown in a pile.

▶ Ask the teens why they thought a phrase was assertive, passive, or aggressive.

Posture Speaks

Understanding how body posture affects communication

Level 2
Types of Communication

What You'll Need: Images of people in different types of postures (happy, defensive, angry, etc.); dry-erase board and markers; tape

Duration: 20 minutes

Best for: 1 to 6 people

Prep: Tape images of common body postures to a dry-erase board.

LEADING THE ACTIVITY

1. Talk about nonverbal communication and how posture and body language play a big role in how we communicate.

2. Provide an example of how posture can contradict what we are trying to communicate. For example, tell the teen(s) you are interested in what they say, but stand with your arms folded across your chest. Ask them what your posture is actually saying.

3. Ask a teen to go to the board, choose a picture, and write the message the posture is conveying next to the picture. Have them explain their answer.

4. Continue this until all images are labeled.

5. Discuss the results.

DISCUSSION QUESTIONS

▸ What images were the most difficult to interpret? Why?

▸ Describe a time when someone's posture made you uncomfortable. What were they doing?

▸ How can you be more mindful of your posture to make sure you are communicating effectively?

PRO TIP

▸ If time allows, give teen(s) an opportunity to act out postures related to emotions. Then let them quickly "fix" the posture so that it conveys respect, confidence, and so on.

Hearing with Your Eyes

Illustrating the influence of nonverbal communication and listening skills

Level 2
Types of Communication

What You'll Need: No materials needed

Duration: 15 minutes

Best for: 4 to 16 people

LEADING THE ACTIVITY

1. Have the teens stand in a line facing you.

2. Give a series of simple directions they can quickly complete. For example, "Hands on hips, touch your toes, put your arms in the air." (You should also follow your directions.)

3. After giving five directions, give another, but don't follow it yourself. For example, say, "Touch your stomach," but put your hands on your forehead.

4. Tell anyone who didn't follow your verbal direction that they are out of the game.

5. Repeat the process until there is only one teen left in line.

6. Have the group discuss the activity.

DISCUSSION QUESTIONS

▶ What challenges did you have during this activity?

▶ Why do you think it may be easier to see something than hear it?

▶ How can being a good listener be especially valuable when there are distractions?

PRO TIPS

▶ If time allows, have teens volunteer to play the role of the facilitator.

▶ Adjust the speed of your directions based on the group's reactions.

▶ Provide plenty of encouragement and positive reinforcement, especially for teens having difficulty being "out."

Using "I" Statements

Practicing "I" statements to help with assertive communication

Level 2
Types of Communication

What You'll Need: Prepared scenarios

Duration: 15 to 20 minutes

Best for: 3 to 8 people

Prep: Print a list of scenarios in which "I" statements would be useful, such as hurt feelings or arguments with parents.

LEADING THE ACTIVITY

1. Discuss how an upsetting or frustrating situation can make it difficult to communicate assertively.

2. Define **"I" statements** as a form of communication that focuses on feelings or views of the speaker—not what the other person is doing. Give examples, such as "I feel upset and disappointed when you are late for our dates."

3. Have two teens come to the front and act out a common frustrating scenario. If necessary, give them a few minutes to plan the role-play.

4. After 1 to 3 minutes, pause the role-play and have the group discuss and provide "I" statements that could be used in the situation.

5. Repeat the process for each scenario as time allows.

DISCUSSION QUESTIONS

▶ What were some examples of negative communication during the role-plays?

▶ How would using more "I" statements have changed how each scenario played out?

▶ What are some advantages of using "I" statements, especially when you are angry, frustrated, or upset?

PRO TIPS

▶ Ensure that the teens aren't crossing any boundaries during role-plays that may be triggers for those dealing with trauma or anger issues.

▶ Feel free to stop a role-play midway through so teens can interject an "I" statement that would change the trajectory of the role-play.

Group Debate

Practicing assertive communication in a group setting

Level 3
Communication in Everyday Life

What You'll Need: No materials needed

Duration: 20 to 30 minutes

Best for: 4 to 12 people

LEADING THE ACTIVITY

1. Split teens into two teams. Explain that they will participate in short debates during which they'll have to argue their team's stance on a topic.

2. Set ground rules before the debates, such as participants must use indoor voices and speak respectfully.

3. Provide a simple debate topic, such as "the weather is nice today," and assign each team a pro or con position. Allow the teams to debate for up to 5 minutes.

4. Next, choose a more challenging subject, like "our school needs a dress code." Allow teams to debate for up to 7 minutes.

5. At appropriate points, pause the debate to point out the teens' positive and negative use of assertive communication.

6. Allow teens to discuss this experience.

DISCUSSION QUESTIONS

▶ What challenges did you encounter while debating topics?

▶ What types of communication appeared to be most effective while debating?

▶ How could assertive communication help you get your point across in everyday life?

PRO TIPS

▶ If you are familiar with the teens in your group, try to have an even distribution of assertive teens on both teams.

▶ Avoid controversial topics. The goal is to practice communication rather than debate "hot topics."

▶ Make sure teens use "I" statements when discussing examples of positive/negative communication to minimize blaming or attacking others.

Eye Contact

Practicing eye contact and understanding its value in everyday communication

Level 3
Communication in Everyday Life

What You'll Need: No materials needed

Duration: 20 minutes

Best for: 4 to 10 people

LEADING THE ACTIVITY

1. Define and discuss eye contact. Have the group brainstorm why it might be important.

2. Pair up the teens and explain they will do a few exercises to practice making eye contact.

3. Ask them to chat about anything for 30 seconds while maintaining eye contact.

4. Next, give them a specific topic and ask them to discuss it for up to 3 minutes while maintaining eye contact.

5. Instruct one teen in each pair to talk about an embarrassing moment while maintaining eye contact. After 1 to 2 minutes, have pairs switch roles.

6. Finally, have teens maintain eye contact without talking for 1 minute.

7. Have the entire group discuss their experiences.

DISCUSSION QUESTIONS

▶ Which eye contact activity was most difficult for you? The easiest?

▶ How did it feel when your partner maintained eye contact while you were speaking?

▶ Why is eye contact an important part of face-to-face communication?

PRO TIPS

▶ Some teens may have difficulty with this exercise. Provide verbal encouragement throughout the activity.

▶ Shorten or lengthen the times of each step of the activity based on your group's skill level.

▶ Discuss how some cultures view eye contact differently.

I Could Use Some Feedback

Giving and receiving feedback to complete a task

Level 3
Communication in Everyday Life

What You'll Need: Pens or pencils; paper

Duration: 20 to 30 minutes

Best for: 2 to 8 people

LEADING THE ACTIVITY

1. Have teens pair up, with one person as the "coach" and the other as the "illustrator."

2. Ask the coach to draw a simple image, like an octagon or a squiggle.

3. Have the coach give the illustrator step-by-step instructions to draw the shape without disclosing what it actually is. Tell the illustrator not to let the coach see the drawing.

4. Allow 2 to 3 minutes for this.

5. Then have the coach look at the drawing and provide feedback about how accurately the drawing depicts the image (without disclosing what the desired image should be).

6. Resume the activity for another 2 to 3 minutes.

7. Allow the pairs to look at the final pictures together and compare them to the desired image.

8. Have them switch roles and repeat the activity using a different image.

DISCUSSION QUESTIONS

▶ For the coaches, did you feel your feedback was helpful?

▶ For the illustrators, what did you feel when you were receiving feedback?

▶ How can giving and receiving feedback help you be more successful?

PRO TIPS

▶ Make sure to monitor how the coaches are providing feedback and how the illustrators are accepting it.

▶ Alter the amount of time and number of feedback sessions based on the skill level needed to draw the object.

Communicating through Play

Exploring communication styles during leisure experiences

Level 3
Communication in Everyday Life

What You'll Need: Material for different simple games (e.g., cards, tic-tac-toe, hangman)

Duration: 15 to 20 minutes

Best for: 4 to 12 people

LEADING THE ACTIVITY

1. Give the teens up to 15 minutes to play some of the games you've provided. Closely observe how they communicate.

2. After the "free play" period, introduce this quote attributed to Plato: "You can learn more about a man in one hour of play than in a lifetime of conversation." Discuss its meaning.

3. Ask them to discuss what they learned about each other while playing the games.

4. Share your observations. For example, "[Name] seems very competitive" or "[Name] likes to make others laugh."

5. Allow them to summarize what they learned about the experience.

DISCUSSION QUESTIONS

▶ Do you agree with the quote from Plato? Why or why not?

▶ Describe a time when you learned more about a person by playing together.

▶ What did you learn about you and your peers' communication during this activity?

PRO TIPS

▶ Provide activities that will interest and engage your teens for up to 15 minutes.

▶ Both competitive and noncompetitive games will work for this activity.

▶ Encourage the teens to use "I" statements when they talk about others in the group.

I'm a Star!

Helping teens deal with their fear of public speaking

Level 3
Communication in Everyday Life

What You'll Need: No materials needed

Duration: 20 minutes

Best for: 3 to 10 people

LEADING THE ACTIVITY

1. Discuss public speaking and how the group feels about it.

2. Have them share some common fears about public speaking and offer them tips for feeling more comfortable.

3. Discuss how public speaking becomes easier with practice. Explain that this exercise is a fun way to get a little practice.

4. Ask for a volunteer to stand in front of the others and begin telling a story. If necessary, provide a prompt to start the story.

5. After 30 seconds, have the speaker pick another person in the group to continue the story.

6. Continue until everyone has had a chance to speak.

7. Discuss how it felt to practice public speaking.

DISCUSSION QUESTIONS

▶ How did you feel talking in front of the group?

▶ What fears do you have while public speaking? Did they come true when you were telling your part of the story?

▶ What have you learned in this session that can help you become a better public speaker?

PRO TIPS

▶ Modify how long each teen tells the story to give more or less practice.

▶ Use prompts that can create a fun, entertaining story. For example, "Bob just found a bag full of weird items while walking down the street. It was filled with ..."

▶ If a teen freezes up in front of the group, provide extra encouragement and prompting to restart the story.

CHAPTER 4

STRESS MANAGEMENT

Stress is a physiological response that arises when we're pushed past our limits or when we feel out of our comfort zones. It can motivate us to do better or cripple us with inaction. The adolescent years are filled with events that consistently challenge the boundaries of a teen's comfort zones.

Learning how to manage stress allows teens to harness this powerful response to think and act more productively. Instead of feeling hopeless or overwhelmed, they can learn to overcome challenges and take new ones in stride.

The activities in this chapter are divided into three levels: Understanding Stress (Level 1), Stress Management Techniques (Level 2), and Reducing Stress in Everyday Life (Level 3). Level 1 activities help teens develop a greater awareness of their stress and how it affects them. Level 2 teaches practical activities to help manage stress. Level 3 activities help teens apply stress management techniques to their daily lives.

Good and Bad Stress

Exploring common stressors and recognizing good versus bad stress

Level 1
Understanding Stress

What You'll Need: Pencils and paper; dry-erase board and markers

Duration: 15 to 20 minutes

Best for: 1 to 6 people

LEADING THE ACTIVITY

1. Define stress and discuss how it is a part of everyday life—especially for teens.

2. Give the teen(s) a couple minutes to reflect on and list stressors in their lives.

3. Define **good stress**, short-term stressors that push us to focus and improve performance, such as starting a new job.

4. Define **bad stress**, chronic stressors that cause anxiety and unpleasant emotions and can decrease performance, such as ongoing family troubles.

5. Divide a dry-erase board into two sections: good stress and bad stress.

6. Ask the teen(s) to list three examples from their own stressor list on the board.

7. Discuss the results of this activity.

DISCUSSION QUESTIONS

▶ How can you tell the difference between good and bad stress?

▶ What common stressors did you notice from this activity?

▶ How can understanding good and bad stress help you cope more effectively?

PRO TIPS

▶ Provide multiple examples of good and bad stress to help the teen(s) grasp the concept.

▶ If the teen(s) are reluctant to discuss their personal stressors, anonymously collect examples and have the teen(s) categorize them.

▶ Explain that people react differently to stress, so each answer depends on the individual.

What's Stressing Me Out?

A game to engage teens and get them to talk about common stressors

Level 1
Understanding Stress

What You'll Need: Balloons; markers

Duration: 15 to 20 minutes

Best for: 3 to 9 people

Prep: Blow up several balloons and use a marker to write a common stressor for teens on each (e.g., school, family, future, relationships).

LEADING THE ACTIVITY

1. Have the teens stand in a circle. Tell them to work together to keep the balloons from touching the floor.

2. Start with one or two balloons and introduce more as the group becomes more comfortable.

3. When a balloon touches the ground, stop the activity and read the word written on it.

4. Ask each teen to give an example of a stressor (personal or generalized) that they associate with that word.

5. Restart the activity and continue until each stressor has been addressed.

DISCUSSION QUESTIONS

▶ How did you feel when more balloons were added to the circle?

▶ What were some of the common stressors the group mentioned?

▶ How can understanding the stressors in your life help you cope more effectively?

PRO TIPS

▶ It's okay if the same balloon hits the ground multiple times—remind teens they can give general answers if they can't come up with personal examples.

▶ Teens can stand closer or farther apart to make the activity more interesting.

▶ While teens are "juggling" balloons, remind them that sometimes stress may seem overwhelming or unmanageable, which is what this game is supposed to represent.

How Stress Affects My Body

Examining how stress manifests in the body

Level 1
Understanding Stress

What You'll Need: Paper; colored pencils (green, yellow, and red)

Duration: 15 to 20 minutes

Best for: 1 to 8 people

LEADING THE ACTIVITY

1. Discuss the different ways stress can affect the body.

2. Ask the teen(s) to reflect on something that stresses them out and notice (without judgment) any tightness, tension, or other sensations in their body (1 to 2 minutes).

3. Have them take a few moments to reorient to the room.

4. Ask them to draw an outline of their body, coloring the areas affected by the stressful situation they thought of. Have them use green for no sensations; yellow for some tightness or tension; and red for significant tightness, tension, or other sensations.

5. Let them share and discuss.

DISCUSSION QUESTIONS

▶ What areas of your body were most affected by stress? What did you feel?

▶ What were some of the most common areas of the body affected by stress?

▶ How can becoming mindful of your body's stress response help you determine stress levels?

PRO TIPS

▶ For the reflection period, focus on moderate stressors to avoid triggering. Provide examples.

▶ Remind teen(s) that there are no right or wrong answers—everyone experiences stress differently.

▶ Without individualized support, this activity may not be appropriate for teens dealing with severe trauma or grief.

Procrastination Stress

Noticing how procrastination can create or exacerbate stress

Level 1
Understanding Stress

What You'll Need: Simple puzzles, word games, or other challenging activities

Duration: 20 to 25 minutes

Best for: 1 to 8 people

LEADING THE ACTIVITY

1. Give each teen a puzzle or other activity and set a time limit that's too short for them to complete the activity.

2. Tell the teen(s) to begin and give them updates as the clock winds down. For example, "You've only got one minute to go." (This helps illustrate the time pressures of procrastination.)

3. Stop the activity when time is up. Ask how they felt.

4. Have the teen(s) find new puzzles or other activities.

5. Restart the clock, this time allowing enough time for completion.

6. Provide more supportive prompts, such as "You're doing well, take your time and focus."

7. Stop the activity when the set time elapses or every teen completes the activity.

8. Discuss how the teen(s) felt this time. Talk about how allowing appropriate time to complete duties can lower their stress.

DISCUSSION QUESTIONS

▶ How did you feel as I counted down the minutes for you to complete the activity?

▶ Was it easier to complete the activity with more time and less stress?

▶ How can procrastination create unnecessary stress in your life?

PRO TIPS

▶ Choose activities that are engaging and challenging for your teens. Puzzles work great, but mazes or "find the difference" activities can also be used.

▶ Monitor the level of frustration after the first part of the activity and provide encouragement to keep them engaged to do the second part.

▶ Consider having teens pair up for larger groups.

Perfection Stress

Understanding how perfectionism leads to stress and helping teens embrace their own "imperfections"

What You'll Need: Dry-erase board and marker

Duration: 15 to 20 minutes

Best for: 2 to 8 people

Level 1
Understanding Stress

LEADING THE ACTIVITY

1. Define perfectionism and discuss how it can cause unrealistic expectations and stress.

2. Develop a list of unrealistic ideals teens face in the pursuit of perfection. Write them on the board.

3. Identify where these expectations come from and write them on another section of the board.

4. Ask for specific examples of how each causes stress.

5. Discuss how acceptance of imperfections and letting go of perfectionism can lead to a more productive, focused life.

6. Ask teens to share an imperfection they accept about themselves.

7. Explain that accepting some imperfections doesn't mean giving up. Rather, it is a chance to celebrate differences and be kinder to yourself.

DISCUSSION QUESTIONS

▶ What expectations are causing you the most stress?

▶ What people, things, or situations make you feel "imperfect"?

▶ How can accepting some of your imperfections help you manage stress?

PRO TIPS

▶ Allow time to discuss what makes certain expectations unrealistic.

▶ Encourage teens to remain respectful when talking about how others create unrealistic expectations.

▶ Some apparently unrealistic expectations, like doing well at school, may actually be attainable. Discuss the difference between unrealistic and high expectations.

Emoji Stress Ball

Making stress balls and learning when they can be helpful

Level 2
Stress Management Techniques

What You'll Need: Balloons; baking soda; hair conditioner; bowls; spoons; scissors; empty plastic water bottles; permanent or dry-erase markers

Duration: 15 to 20 minutes

Best for: 1 to 6 people

Prep: Make a stress ball ahead of time to serve as an example of the finished project.

LEADING THE ACTIVITY

1. Discuss how stress balls can help release nervous energy, allow you to refocus, and curb stress hormones.

2. Ask the teen(s) to create their own stress balls as you demonstrate:

   - Place two cups of baking soda in a bowl.
   - Add about half a cup of hair conditioner and mix together.
   - Cut off the top third of an empty plastic water bottle. (This will be the funnel.)
   - Attach the balloon to the bottle opening.
   - Add the baking soda/hair conditioner mixture to the other end of the cut bottle.
   - Push the mixture into the balloon with the spoon.
   - Ensure that there are no air bubbles in the balloon and tie it closed.
   - Use markers to decorate with an emoji.

DISCUSSION QUESTIONS

▶ What emoji did you use for your stress ball? Why?

▶ When might a stress ball help you manage or refocus stress?

PRO TIPS

▶ The amount of hair conditioner used determines how squishy the stress ball will be.

▶ Spend time discussing the benefits of the stress ball and good times to use it.

Three Coping Skills

Learning some simple
stress-management skills

Level 2
Stress Management
Techniques

What You'll Need: Pencils; paper; yoga mats (if available)

Duration: 15 to 20 minutes

Best for: 1 to 8 people

LEADING THE ACTIVITY

1. Discuss what teens do when they're feeling stressed. Define **coping skills** as a person's deliberate methods to deal with stressful situations. Provide some examples.

2. Introduce these coping skills and give the teen(s) a chance to practice them:

    -   **Journaling:** Explain that writing down stressors can help us process our thoughts and emotions. Have them write about a stressful situation for 3 to 4 minutes.

    -   **Simple yoga pose:** If space allows, have them practice the "corpse" pose. Have them lie on their backs with their legs close together but not touching. Arms should be at the sides with palms up. Eyes are closed (if comfortable). Let them practice this pose for 3 to 5 minutes while focusing on their breath and briefly paying attention to each part of the body.

    -   **To-do lists:** Explain how this common activity can actually help beat stress by breaking down overwhelming situations into manageable chunks. You also get to enjoy a small victory when each item is completed.

DISCUSSION QUESTIONS

▶ Which coping skill was most effective?

▶ How can incorporating coping skills into your daily routine help you manage stress and improve your mood?

PRO TIPS

▶ Allow more or less time on each activity based on the group's progress.

▶ Feel free to use alternative coping skills that you feel will resonate better with your teens.

▶ If time allows, have teens demonstrate their own ideas for positive coping skills.

Progressive Relaxation

Learning a relaxation technique to help manage stress

Level 2
Stress Management Techniques

What You'll Need: No materials needed

Duration: 20 to 25 minutes

Best for: 1 to 5 people

LEADING THE ACTIVITY

1. Discuss some of the physical and mental effects we feel when stressed out. Ask the teen(s) how relaxation can reduce stress and what they do to relax.

2. Give them a minute or two to reflect on how they are feeling right now. Have them rate their stress level from 1 to 5 (5 being very stressed out).

3. Guide them through the following **progressive relaxation exercise**.

   - Settle into a comfortable position (standing or lying down).

   - Focus on your breath for a minute or two, just inhaling and exhaling.

   - Imagine a calming ball of light just above your head. It can be any color you want.

   - The ball of light starts pouring into your body through the top of your head.

   - Imagine your feet being filled with this light and relaxing, and then your ankles being filled.... (Continue naming body parts until the body is completely filled with this calming light.)

   - Spend a minute just observing your body filled with this calming light.

   - Take a couple of deep breaths and reorient yourself to the room.

DISCUSSION QUESTIONS

▸ Describe how you felt during the activity.

▸ What differences did you notice in your body after the activity?

▸ Give some examples of when this relaxation technique can be useful for you.

PRO TIPS

▸ Guide the teen(s) with a slow, calm voice. Play calming music if desired.

▸ Remind teen(s) that distractions, like thoughts, are normal, and they should just return to the exercise.

Letting Go of Stress

Releasing tension and improving overall mental well-being by letting go of stressors

Level 2
Stress Management Techniques

What You'll Need: Rope

Duration: 20 to 30 minutes

Best for: 3 to 9 people

LEADING THE ACTIVITY

1. Discuss how focusing too much on stressors can exacerbate them and increase tension in the body.

2. Give one end of a rope to a teen. Ask them to briefly describe a cause of their stress.

3. Have one or two peers grab the other end of the rope and gently pull.

4. Ask the teen to talk more about this stressor as their peers pull a little harder on the rope.

5. Ask the teen if they are ready to let go of this stress.

6. If the answer is "no," allow more discussion about the stress. Have the peers pull a little harder on the rope.

7. Ask again about letting go of stress. When they answer "yes," have the peers ease tension, and then ask the teen to gently let go of the rope.

8. Have the teen describe how it felt when they symbolically let go of a stressor.

9. Repeat the exercise with others in the group.

DISCUSSION QUESTIONS

▸ How did it feel talking about your stress while others were pulling on the rope?

▸ What was the first thing you thought about when the rope was released?

▸ Which one of your stressors do you think you can start letting go of today?

PRO TIPS

▸ Hold the session in a safe room with enough space to avoid bumping into any objects when the teen lets go of the rope.

▸ Instruct teens not to pull too hard on the rope or let go too quickly.

▸ Offer encouragement or guided questions while talking about the stressor.

Using Leisure to Beat Stress

Exploring positive leisure activities to cope with stress and nurture the body/mind

Level 2
Stress Management Techniques

What You'll Need: Pencils and paper

Duration: 20 to 25 minutes

Best for: 2 to 8 people

LEADING THE ACTIVITY

1. Discuss that how we choose to spend our free time can diminish stress and improve well-being.

2. Have teens list at least seven favorite leisure activities on a piece of paper.

3. Have them add a "+" next to the positive activities and a "−" by the negative ones.

4. Then have them place a star by any of the activities that help relieve stress.

5. Allow them to discuss their top stress-relieving activities and how they help.

6. On the other side of the paper, have them make a plan to use a positive leisure activity next time they are stressed out.

7. Have them start with: "Next time I am stressed out, I can _____."

8. Then have them describe the specific steps they will take. For example, "I will call a friend, walk to the park, and play a game of one-on-one basketball."

DISCUSSION QUESTIONS

▶ What do you find yourself doing most often when you are stressed out?

▶ How can leisure activities help with your stress? Which ones actually add stress?

▶ How can an actionable plan help when you feel overwhelmed by your emotions?

PRO TIPS

▶ At the beginning of the activity, review what leisure means and have teens come up with examples of leisure activities.

▶ Allow teens to talk about how their favorite activities benefit them aside from managing stress. Tie in how these benefits can also help with stress and overall health.

Worries About the Future

Examining and troubleshooting teens' stressors about the future

Level 3
Reducing Stress in Everyday Life

What You'll Need: Paper; pencils; different-colored highlighters

Duration: 20 to 25 minutes

Best for: 1 to 5 people

LEADING THE ACTIVITY

1. Discuss how worries about the future can cause anxiety and stress.

2. Talk about which worries and stress teens can and cannot control.

3. Have teen(s) divide a piece of paper into four sections and label them *Tomorrow, Next week, Next month,* and *Next year.*

4. Give them a few minutes to brainstorm and write down things that may be causing stress in each category.

5. Have them highlight things they might be able to control with one color and those they can't control with another. Don't highlight the stressors they are uncertain about.

6. Allow them to share and discuss their lists.

7. Have them pick three of the stressors they have some control over and write down things they can do to reduce the stress.

DISCUSSION QUESTIONS

▸ What worries you most about the future, and why?

▸ How can you cope with the things you cannot control?

▸ What steps can you start today to help reduce stress about the future?

PRO TIPS

▸ Provide prompts to help teens come up with stressors for each category.

▸ Remind teen(s) there are no wrong answers: Everyone experiences stress differently.

Family Pressures

Helping teens identify and discuss difficult family situations

Level 3
Reducing Stress in Everyday Life

What You'll Need: Paper; pencils; colored pencils

Duration: 15 to 25 minutes

Best for: 2 to 5 people

LEADING THE ACTIVITY

1. Talk about how family members and dynamics can be a source of stress. Have the teens provide examples.

2. Ask them to draw a picture of everyone in their family and create dialogue bubbles about things each family member says or does that cause them stress.

3. Share and discuss the intentions of each family member. For example, "My dad keeps bothering me about my grades. I think he wants me to go to a good college and be successful."

4. Ask teens to troubleshoot ways to handle family members in these situations and brainstorm healthy ways to relieve stress.

DISCUSSION QUESTIONS

▶ Which member of your family causes you the most stress? Why?

▶ What are some ways you can communicate with this person more effectively?

▶ When you feel stressed out by your family, what are some positive things you can do to feel better?

PRO TIPS

▶ Have teens come to their own conclusions about their family situations with guided questions.

▶ Encourage teens to use "I" statements when talking about family members.

▶ Discuss how we can't control how others act, just how we react. Also note that sometimes these reactions may be causing additional stress.

▶ Take time to discuss some of the positive aspects of difficult family members.

Peer Pressures

Exploring common ways peers cause stress in everyday life

Level 3
Reducing Stress in Everyday Life

What You'll Need: Note cards (six per person); pencils

Duration: 20 to 30 minutes

Best for: 2 to 8 people

LEADING THE ACTIVITY

1. Discuss how peers can have a positive or negative influence on our stress levels. Have the teens brainstorm some examples.

2. Give each teen six note cards and a pencil. Ask them to write what their peers do that cause them stress.

3. Collect the note cards and shuffle them, keeping the answers anonymous.

4. Read the responses on each card and have the teens rate how much these situations stress them out on a scale of 1 to 5 (5 being the most stressful).

5. Discuss the most common answers and any unique situations that may be causing stress.

DISCUSSION QUESTIONS

▶ How much of your stress is due to your peers? Why do you think that is?

▶ What are some ways you can minimize the stress caused by peers?

▶ How can understanding stress caused by peers allow you to manage it more effectively?

PRO TIPS

▶ Feel free to modify the number of cards a teen should fill out.

▶ Intervene if anyone belittles someone else's answers. Explain that teens feel stress in many different ways and even seemingly insignificant matters can cause a lot of stress.

▶ If bullying is a common issue, refer to chapter 8 in this book for more activity ideas.

Becoming Stress-Proof

Learning how taking care of the body builds resilience to stress

Level 3
Reducing Stress in Everyday Life

What You'll Need: Large pieces of paper or poster board; pencils; colored pencils or markers

Duration: 20 to 25 minutes

Best for: 1 to 6 people

LEADING THE ACTIVITY

1. Discuss how taking care of their body can make teen(s) more resilient to stress.

2. Have the teen(s) brainstorm some ways self-care can help us feel better mentally and physically.

3. Have them come up with a stress-proof superhero and make a poster, showcasing those self-care powers that make the superhero resilient to different stressors. (For group sessions, have the teens collaborate on the superhero's outfit and the powers gained from self-care.)

4. Have the teen(s) present their poster and talk about which self-care strategies they believe to be most effective.

DISCUSSION QUESTIONS

▶ What are some ways you can become more stress-proof?

▶ Give an example of when not taking proper care of yourself caused you to react negatively to stress.

▶ What is one self-care strategy you can start using today?

PRO TIPS

▶ If a superhero theme isn't appropriate for the group, instead have the teen(s) make posters of themselves becoming stress-proof.

▶ After the activity, discuss how being stress-proof isn't actually a superpower but a result of better self-care routines.

▶ Remind the teen(s) that stress is common but how they respond can lessen its effects.

Study to Stress Less

Learning successful
study skills and pre-exam
time management

What You'll Need: Pencils and paper

Duration: 20 to 25 minutes

Best for: 1 to 6 people

Level 3
Reducing Stress in
Everyday Life

LEADING THE ACTIVITY

1. Discuss how the teen(s) feel right before a big exam and how they study for tests.

2. Talk about how successful study habits can help reduce pre-exam stress. Have them brainstorm some effective study habits.

3. Provide additional tips for making studying more effective, such as eliminating distractions, staying healthy, and using memory games like mnemonic devices.

4. Have them write the answers to the following questions:

    -   What does my ideal study space look like?

    -   How long do I plan to devote each day to studying?

    -   How can I reward myself for a productive study session?

    -   What studying tips have I found to be the most helpful?

5. Ask them to use their answers to create a study schedule for the week leading up to the next big test. Let them share answers and schedules.

DISCUSSION QUESTIONS

▶ Do you think studying is important? Why or why not?

▶ What studying tips did you find most useful from this activity?

▶ How can sticking to your study schedule reduce stress prior to taking a test?

PRO TIPS

▶ Before you provide extra tips, be sure to allow teen(s) to come up with as many positive study habits as possible on their own.

▶ Acknowledge that each student learns differently, so some tips may feel more effective than others.

▶ If time permits, discuss habits that may make studying unproductive.

CHAPTER 5

ANGER MANAGEMENT

Anger is a natural, often intense emotion that results from feeling provoked or wronged. It's not just a state of mind; anger can also be felt throughout the body. Anger can motivate us to change negative aspects of our lives, but it can also lead to rash, impulsive behaviors that do more harm than good.

Anger is especially hard for teens to deal with because their emotions are amplified. They're still learning how to rationally cope with triggering situations. Teens who don't know how to release their anger in healthy ways may act out and then face major consequences. Practicing anger management gives teens concrete tools to deal with their negative feelings productively.

The activities in this chapter are divided into three levels: Understanding Anger (Level 1), A Closer Look at Anger (Level 2), and Reducing Anger (Level 3). Level 1 activities give teens a chance to personally define anger and see its effect on the mind and body. Level 2 helps teens discover the sources of their anger and become more aware of their relationship with anger. Level 3 activities help teens cope with anger and make it feel less overwhelming in the moment.

How I React to Anger

Noticing positive and
negative reactions
to anger

What You'll Need: Pencils and paper

Duration: 15 to 20 minutes

Best for: 1 to 8 people

Level 1
Understanding Anger

LEADING THE ACTIVITY

1. Have the teen(s) define anger. Discuss common ways people react to anger.

2. Ask them to divide a piece of paper into six different sections.

3. In each section have them write one way they react to anger.

4. Have the teen(s) determine if each reaction is a positive or negative way to deal with anger.

5. Allow them to share and discuss their findings.

6. For the negative reactions, ask the teen(s) to come up with a similar, more positive reaction.

7. Discuss the positive alternatives.

DISCUSSION QUESTIONS

▶ What do you feel is the most positive way you deal with anger? Most negative?

▶ How can you change your negative reactions?

▶ How can noticing how you react to anger now help you deal with anger in the future?

PRO TIPS

▶ Feel free to divide the paper into more or fewer sections depending on your group's abilities.

▶ If they are having trouble coming up with anger coping skills, brainstorm a list together.

▶ Remind teen(s) that everyone deals with and reacts to anger differently.

What Triggers My Anger?

Exploring sources of anger

Level 1
Understanding Anger

What You'll Need: Pencils and paper

Duration: 15 to 20 minutes

Best for: 1 to 8 people

LEADING THE ACTIVITY

1. Define **anger triggers** as the people, places, or situations that cause a person to feel mad, irritated, or angry.

2. Have the teen(s) brainstorm common anger triggers.

3. Discuss how even very common situations like being hungry, annoyed, lonely, or tired—sometimes known as HALT—can contribute to anger.

4. Instruct teen(s) to write down as many triggers as they can think for these three categories: people, places, and situations.

5. After brainstorming, have them pick their top five anger triggers and share.

6. Discuss the findings.

DISCUSSION QUESTIONS

▶ What were some of the most common anger triggers discussed today?

▶ While brainstorming your triggers, what were some surprising answers you came up with?

▶ How can recognizing your anger triggers help you manage anger in the future?

PRO TIPS

▶ Taking extra time to brainstorm each individual category may yield more ideas.

▶ Provide examples for each category to help generate ideas.

▶ Remind the teen(s) there are no right or wrong answers. Many factors contribute to a person's anger.

Acting Out

Identifying productive ways to release anger

Level 1
Understanding Anger

What You'll Need: Some props for role-playing (if available)

Duration: 15 to 20 minutes

Best for: 2 to 10 people

LEADING THE ACTIVITY

1. Discuss how people often deal with anger. Ask the teens to provide both positive and negative examples of releasing anger.

2. Ask them to pair up.

3. Give each pair a common scenario, such as being ignored or disrespected, in which someone would act out in anger. Tell them to highlight negatively releasing anger.

4. Let them take a few minutes to discuss their role-plays.

5. Give 1 to 3 minutes for each role-play.

6. After each role-play, discuss how the situation could have been handled more appropriately.

DISCUSSION QUESTIONS

▶ What were some of the common ways you saw people act out today?

▶ How did it feel when someone acted out toward you?

▶ Which role-plays were the most surprising? Why?

▶ How can finding productive ways to deal with acting-out behavior allow you to handle a situation more calmly?

PRO TIPS

▶ Set ground rules (such as minding others' personal space) for the role-play to ensure respect, safety, and security of everyone in the group.

▶ Stop the role-play if you believe someone is becoming upset or is crossing the boundaries set by your ground rules.

▶ Give prompts and ideas to encourage pairs to come up with elaborate role-plays and not just generic examples.

The Anger Inside Me

Exploring what anger feels like in the body

Understanding Anger

What You'll Need: Pencils; paper; colored pencils (red)

Duration: 15 to 20 minutes

Best for: 1 to 6 people

LEADING THE ACTIVITY

1. Discuss how everyone feels anger differently. Ask the teen(s) to list some ways anger manifests in the body.

2. Have them draw an outline of their body on a piece of paper.

3. Ask them to quietly think about a situation that makes them angry, mindfully noticing how they feel in every area of their body.

4. Have them color their body outlines red in any area that felt affected by anger.

5. Ask them to label what happened in each red area. For example, "My fists clenched."

6. Allow them to discuss and share their drawings.

DISCUSSION QUESTIONS

▶ Describe how your body feels anger.

▶ What was a common area of the body where people felt anger?

▶ How can understanding the effects of anger on the body help you become more aware of this emotion in the future?

PRO TIPS

▶ During the quiet reflection period, prompt teens to imagine the angry situation with all of their senses to help make the visualization more realistic.

▶ Add more colors to help the teen(s) identify different levels of anger in the body.

▶ If a teen has a hard time defining areas of the body, encourage them to take the outline home and color it in when they become angry or irritated.

The Scream

Identifying potential sources of anger

Level 1
Understanding Anger

What You'll Need: A copy of Edvard Munch's *The Scream* painting; paper and pencils; colored pencils or markers

Duration: 20 to 25 minutes

Best for: 1 to 6 people

LEADING THE ACTIVITY

1. Identify some potential sources of anger many teens face. Have the teen(s) brainstorm additional ideas.

2. Present the image of Edvard Munch's painting *The Scream*. Ask the teen(s) to describe what is going on in this painting.

3. Encourage them to share a time when they felt like the person in the painting.

4. Instruct them to create their own version of this image using available art materials.

5. Somewhere on their drawing, ask them to write down the source of their own anger that made them feel like the person in their *Scream*.

6. Allow them to share and discuss.

DISCUSSION QUESTIONS

▶ Talk about a time you felt like the person in this painting.

▶ Why do you think people use art to portray emotions like anger?

▶ How can knowing your sources of anger help prevent you from being overcome with emotions?

PRO TIPS

▶ Consider using other images and artwork to help facilitate ideas.

▶ Encourage the teen(s) to incorporate their sources of anger into their drawing, as opposed to just writing them down.

▶ Provide as many art materials as possible to keep teen(s) engaged.

The Consequences of My Anger

Visualizing the ramifications of acting out in anger

Level 2
A Closer Look at Anger

What You'll Need: Paper; pencils; colored pencils; markers

Duration: 20 to 25 minutes

Best for: 1 to 6 people

LEADING THE ACTIVITY

1. Talk about how people act out when they are angry. Encourage the teen(s) to discuss both positive and negative ways people express anger.

2. Have them think of a time when they expressed their anger negatively and what happened as a result.

3. Have them create a short comic strip illustrating how they acted out negatively and what the consequences were.

4. Then have them create a comic strip illustrating the same situation but expressing anger more positively and the result of that.

5. Share and discuss the comic strips.

DISCUSSION QUESTIONS

▶ Why do you think you chose to act out the way you did in the past?

▶ What other negative consequences has your anger caused?

▶ How can understanding the consequences of your past anger help you make better choices in the future?

PRO TIPS

▶ Provide a comic book template with up to five frames as an example.

▶ Discuss how we can't change the past but can learn from our mistakes and regrets.

▶ If necessary, let the teen(s) talk about the situation they want to draw beforehand to help flesh out ideas.

Social Media Angst

Exploring how popular
social media platforms
can contribute to anger

Level 2
A Closer Look at Anger

What You'll Need: Pencils and paper

Duration: 15 to 25 minutes

Best for: 1 to 6 people

LEADING THE ACTIVITY

1. Ask the teen(s) to name their favorite social media outlets and discuss how much time they spend on each platform.

2. Discuss emotions the teen(s) usually feel while using social media.

3. Have them give examples of how social media may be contributing to their anger.

4. With paper and pencil, have them create sample social media posts that may make them angry, irritated, or frustrated.

5. Allow them to share their posts and talk about why each makes them angry.

6. Summarize and discuss the group's findings.

DISCUSSION QUESTIONS

▶ What are some benefits of using social media?

▶ What do you typically do when a post makes you angry?

▶ What are some positive ways you can handle anger when faced with upsetting social media posts?

PRO TIPS

▶ The teen(s) can write or draw posts—whichever they find most useful.

▶ Allow them to use examples of real or made-up posts.

▶ If posts contain inappropriate or hateful language, discuss why this is ineffective communication.

Anger Bullseyes

Defining and understanding the sources and intensity of anger

Level 2
A Closer Look at Anger

What You'll Need: Dry-erase board or large poster board; sticky notes; pencils; dry-erase markers

Duration: 20 to 30 minutes

Best for: 2 to 8 people

Prep: Draw a large bullseye with five rings on a dry-erase board or poster. Each ring will symbolize a different level of anger.

LEADING THE ACTIVITY

1. Discuss anger and its varying levels of intensity. Have teens identify five levels of anger for the bullseye—for example, irritated, frustrated, upset, mad, and enraged.

2. Clearly define and provide examples for each level of anger with the group.

3. Discuss the meaning of anger triggers. Have teens write down at least five anger triggers, each on a separate sticky note.

4. In turn, have them share one of their sticky notes and then place it on the ring to which it corresponds.

5. Continue until all sticky notes are placed on the board or the allotted time runs out.

6. Summarize and discuss the activity.

DISCUSSION QUESTIONS

▶ What were some of the most common anger triggers?

▶ What made you feel the angriest?

▶ How can identifying sources and intensity of anger help you cope better in the future?

PRO TIPS

▶ Use more or fewer rings on the bullseye to accommodate the group's needs.

▶ Discuss how some triggers may cause more or less anger at different times.

▶ Remind teens that everyone experiences anger differently, so there are no right or wrong answers.

Anger Gauge

Understanding the
physical signs of anger

Level 2
A Closer Look at Anger

What You'll Need: Large piece of paper; colored pencils
or markers

Duration: 15 to 20 minutes

Best for: 1 to 6 people

Prep: Create a sample anger gauge to help teens better
understand the concept.

LEADING THE ACTIVITY

1. Describe the physical feelings teens experience when they are angry. If necessary, name every area of the body and have the teen(s) talk about how anger affects it.

2. On large pieces of paper, have teen(s) draw a fuel gauge, using colors that best represent their feelings. The far-left side should represent calm, and the far-right side intense anger.

3. Have them label each color a different level of anger, such as *Irritated* or *Furious*.

4. Give them a few minutes to reflect on how anger affects them physically.

5. Have them write these symptoms in the appropriate sections of the gauge— for example, "flushed face" in the *Frustrated* section.

6. Discuss the findings of the group.

DISCUSSION QUESTIONS

▶ What are some of the first physical signs that you are experiencing anger?

▶ What physical signs can alert you that your anger may be getting out of control?

▶ How can understanding these signs help you better manage your anger in the future?

PRO TIPS

▶ If teen(s) are having difficulty locating the source of anger, revisit a situation that angered them. Guide them through the situation as they focus on how their body felt.

More Than Just "Mad"

Expanding emotional vocabulary to help release anger in healthy ways

Level 2
A Closer Look at Anger

What You'll Need: Dry-erase board and markers; pencils; paper

Duration: 15 to 20 minutes

Best for: 1 to 6 people

Prep: Create a list of words describing emotions and make a copy for each participant.

LEADING THE ACTIVITY

1. Have the teen(s) give their own definition of anger.

2. Explain that anger can be a blanket term for a variety of unfavorable emotions.

3. Brainstorm words that relate to anger (e.g., *insulted, disgusted, frustrated*) and write them on the board.

4. Have each teen pick five of these words and define them.

5. Then have them write down an example of when they experienced these emotions.

6. Share definitions and examples.

7. Talk about the importance of building an emotional vocabulary. Give each teen the list of emotions that you prepared.

DISCUSSION QUESTIONS

▶ What other emotions do you feel most often when you are "angry"?

▶ How has looking at these different emotions changed your perspective of anger?

▶ How can having a larger emotional vocabulary help reduce anger and frustration?

PRO TIPS

▶ If necessary, provide your prepared list of emotions during the activity to help teens brainstorm more ideas.

▶ If you have additional time, allow teens to role-play specific emotions.

▶ If teen(s) are having difficulty coming up with their own definitions for emotions, just have them provide additional examples as these emotions arise.

Stop . . . Breathe . . . Relief

Reducing the intensity
of anger through
breathing techniques

Level 3
Reducing Anger

What You'll Need: No materials needed

Duration: 15 to 20 minutes

Best for: 1 to 6 people

LEADING THE ACTIVITY

1. Introduce breathing exercises as a way to calm the body and mind.

2. Guide the teen(s) through the following two 3- to 5-minute breathing exercises.
    For both exercises, have them sit in a comfortable position, take a couple of deep
    breaths, and close their eyes if they choose.

    -   Exercise 1: Have the teen(s) quietly count to 4 while inhaling, hold the breath
        for a count of 7, and then slowly exhale while counting to 8. Repeat as long
        as necessary.

    -   Exercise 2: While taking deep breaths, have them picture a word, phrase, or
        image such as "calm" or "I am in control." If their minds wander, tell them to
        acknowledge the thought, let it go, and return focus to the word or image.

3. Have the teen(s) discuss how both exercises felt.

4. Remind them these can be practiced anytime and that practicing them when
    you're not angry will help them work better when you are angry.

DISCUSSION QUESTIONS

▶   Describe how you felt while you were doing these exercises.

▶   What differences did you notice in your mind or body afterward?

▶   When do you think breathing exercises may be helpful?

PRO TIPS

▶   Remind teen(s) it's normal for the mind to wander, especially when first attempting
    breathing exercises.

▶   Consider incorporating these exercises before or after other activities to help
    the group feel more calm and grounded.

▶   Encourage teen(s) to keep a journal about when they practiced these breathing
    techniques and how they felt afterward.

My Cool-Down Spot

An opportunity for teens to make plans for a "time-out" spot in their home

What You'll Need: Pencils and paper

Duration: 15 to 25 minutes

Best for: 1 to 6 people

Level 3
Reducing Anger

LEADING THE ACTIVITY

1. Talk about the importance of taking a time-out or walking away from a troubling situation.

2. Have the teen(s) list things that calm them down when they're angry.

3. Instruct them to plan an "ultimate" cool-down spot in their home. They can draw and/or list things to make the area more calming.

4. Provide prompts like "Are there any items that help you feel calmer?"

5. Allow them to share their cool-down spots and discuss.

DISCUSSION QUESTIONS

▶ What are some of the most important items and activities you would include in your cool-down spot?

▶ How easy would it be to create the cool-down spot you planned?

▶ Why is it important to have calming items and activities available when you are feeling angry?

PRO TIPS

▶ Encourage the teen(s) to be as specific as possible in describing their cool-down spots.

▶ Suggest that they include items they already have or can easily obtain.

▶ Have them discuss why the items and activities help them calm down.

Calm-Down Playlist

Discovering the power of music to release anger

Level 3
Reducing Anger

What You'll Need: Pencils and paper

Duration: 15 to 25 minutes

Best for: 1 to 6 people

LEADING THE ACTIVITY

1. Have the teen(s) discuss their favorite musicians and give reasons why they like these artists.

2. Talk about how music can help us calm down, process emotions, and release anger in a productive way.

3. Have each teen name one "go-to" song for when they are feeling angry or frustrated. Allow them to talk about how this song helps them.

4. Instruct them to list 10 songs for a calm-down playlist and write down why they chose each song.

5. Have them share their playlists and discuss.

DISCUSSION QUESTIONS

▶ How does music help you deal with anger?

▶ What were some great song choices you heard from others in the group?

▶ How can having an anger playlist available prevent you from acting out in more negative ways?

PRO TIPS

▶ Angry or extreme music may actually give teens a productive outlet when they're feeling angry. Don't discourage extreme music unless it is offensive or demeaning to others in the group.

▶ If a teen can't think of a specific song, let them list artists or genres that may help.

▶ If time and resources allow, have teen(s) look up different songs for their playlist on the internet.

Responding to Anger

Exploring alternative ways of responding to anger

Level 3
Reducing Anger

What You'll Need: Pencils; paper; dry-erase board and markers

Duration: 20 to 25 minutes

Best for: 1 to 5 people

LEADING THE ACTIVITY

1. Define **aggression** as a type of behavior that can harm oneself and others. Ask the teen(s) to provide examples of when anger causes aggressive behaviors.

2. Explain that anger is a normal human emotion, but we can respond to it in nonaggressive ways.

3. On a piece of paper, have the teen(s) list five situations that make them angry, leaving space between each example.

4. Brainstorm healthy or positive ways to respond to anger. Discuss the type of anger-provoking situations these positive approaches could help with.

5. Under each situation the teen(s) wrote down, have them complete this statement: "When I am angry because [situation listed], instead of acting out aggressively, I can..."

6. Let them share some statements and discuss.

DISCUSSION QUESTIONS

▶ What are some nonaggressive actions you learned during this session?

▶ Name a time when you acted out aggressively because you weren't sure what else to do with your anger.

▶ How can having a plan in place help prevent you from acting aggressively in the future?

PRO TIPS

▶ During brainstorming, provide different anger-reducing categories to help facilitate ideas (e.g., calming activities, diverting activities, leisure activities).

▶ Remind the teen(s) not every calming strategy will work in every situation, so having several alternatives is a good idea.

It's Not You

Communicating anger
in productive ways

What You'll Need: No materials needed

Duration: 15 to 25 minutes

Level 3
Reducing Anger

Best for: 2 to 8 people

LEADING THE ACTIVITY

1. Have the teens name some of their common anger triggers and give examples of how they handle them.

2. Introduce "I" statements; discuss how they help us effectively communicate thoughts and feelings. (Omit this step if the teens have experience with "I" statements.)

3. Have the teens pair up in groups of two or three.

4. Assign each group a common anger-producing scenario. Allow a few minutes for them to discuss how to act it out.

5. Give each group a turn to act out their scenario.

6. Toward the end of each scenario (or whenever appropriate), pause the acting and ask one of the teens to replace something they said with an "I" statement.

7. Continue the role-play and see if the trajectory changes.

8. Discuss what role "I" statements played in each scenario.

DISCUSSION QUESTIONS

► How did "I" statements change the course of each role-play?

► Why do you think it is so difficult to communicate effectively when angry?

► How can communicating your thoughts and emotions using "I" statements help reduce your anger?

PRO TIPS

► Give several examples of "I" statements, especially if this is new to the teens. Contrast these with "You" statements for further clarification.

► If possible, create scenarios based on the answers teens give in the first step to keep them more invested.

CHAPTER 6

ANXIETY

Anxiety is a frequent and persistent feeling of worry or nervousness about real or perceived outcomes to everyday situations. Anxiety can keep teens from enjoying life and all it has to offer, crippling healthy development.

Teens with persistent anxiety can feel isolated and stuck in a cycle of intrusive thoughts and compulsive behaviors. The activities in this chapter can help teens work through their anxieties and learn practical techniques to keep them at bay.

The activities in this chapter are divided into three levels: Understanding Anxiety (Level 1), How Anxiety Affects Me (Level 2), and Ways to Cope with Anxiety (Level 3). Level 1 activities allow teens to take a closer look at anxiety and what may be causing it. Level 2 activities help teens become aware of the effects of anxiety on their own lives. Finally, Level 3 activities provide practical approaches for managing the symptoms of anxiety.

Anxiety Portrait

Defining and exploring
personal anxiety

Level 1
Understanding Anxiety

What You'll Need: Pencils; paper; colored pencils; markers;
glue; old magazines or printed images that depict anxiety

Duration: 20 to 25 minutes

Best for: 1 to 6 people

LEADING THE ACTIVITY

1. Have the teen(s) define anxiety in their own words. Discuss how anxiety can
   be experienced in many ways.

2. Give the teen(s) a few minutes to reflect on what anxiety means to them and
   how it affects them.

3. Have them spend 15 minutes creating their own portrait of anxiety using the
   supplies you provide.

4. While they are creating their portraits, prompt them to help generate ideas.
   For example, "What does anxiety look like to you?"

5. Allow the teen(s) to display and talk about their anxiety portraits.

6. Discuss the findings.

DISCUSSION QUESTIONS

▶ How did the artwork help you define your personal anxiety?

▶ What insights did you get while creating your portrait?

▶ How can naming your anxiety help reduce it in the future?

PRO TIPS

▶ Encourage the teen(s) to use whatever ideas come to mind—there are no right
  or wrong portraits.

▶ If a teen feels too anxious to present their portrait, have them just say a few
  sentences about it.

▶ Provide as many images, old magazines, and art supplies as possible to help
  stimulate ideas.

My Top Five Worries

Taking a closer look at worries and evaluating them

Level 1
Understanding Anxiety

What You'll Need: Pencils and paper

Duration: 15 to 20 minutes

Best for: 1 to 6 people

LEADING THE ACTIVITY

1. Discuss how anxiety and worries can make it hard to function in everyday life. Have the teen(s) brainstorm ways that anxiety impacts their lives.

2. Discuss how becoming more familiar with particular worries can help identify sources of anxiety.

3. For 2 minutes, have them list any worries that come to mind.

4. Then have them review the list, pick their "Top Five" worries, write them down on a separate piece of paper, and list any thoughts associated with each.

5. Share and discuss their "Top Five" worries.

DISCUSSION QUESTIONS

▶ What are some of your biggest worries?

▶ What worries do you share with others in the group?

▶ How can evaluating your worries be one of the first steps in managing anxiety?

PRO TIPS

▶ During the brainstorm, give prompts to help generate ideas. For example, "What worries you most about school?"

▶ Feel free to list worries on a dry-erase board if available.

▶ Point out that every worry is valid.

My Anxiety Roadmap

Defining and discussing anxiety triggers

Level 1
Understanding Anxiety

What You'll Need: Pencils; paper; colored pencils or markers

Duration: 20 to 25 minutes

Best for: 1 to 5 people

LEADING THE ACTIVITY

1. Discuss how certain people, places, and situations can trigger anxious thoughts or make them worse.

2. Brainstorm examples of external triggers for anxiety (e.g., school, a parent, a bully).

3. Instruct the teen(s) to create a "roadmap" of their anxiety. Have them start with their home (the "you are here" spot) and branch out to other areas of their lives that trigger anxiety.

4. Encourage them to use different colors to represent the level of anxiety caused.

5. Ask them to list why these checkpoints cause anxiety.

6. Have them create an alternative route (if possible) on the map, which would let them avoid certain triggers.

7. Allow them to share their roadmap and discuss findings.

DISCUSSION QUESTIONS

▶ Which spots on your roadmap cause the most anxiety? Why?

▶ Did you notice any recurring themes on your roadmap?

▶ How can defining your anxiety triggers help you reduce anxiety in your life?

PRO TIPS

▶ Tell the teen(s) the map is more symbolic than realistic. Encourage them to get creative by making it look like a lost treasure map or a maze.

▶ Discuss how "alternative routes" aren't always an option (for example, they can't avoid school altogether) but identifying triggers can help them better understand anxiety.

▶ Provide a visual example of an anxiety roadmap to give teens a better idea of what is expected.

Anxiety: Not Just Thoughts

Exploring what anxiety feels like in the body

Level 1
Understanding Anxiety

What You'll Need: Pencils and paper; dry-erase board; a different-colored dry-erase marker for each participant

Duration: 15 to 20 minutes

Best for: 2 to 6 people

LEADING THE ACTIVITY

1. Explain that anxiety is not just thoughts and that it has real physical symptoms.

2. Ask the teens to give examples of how anxiety manifests in the body.

3. Give them a few minutes to think about a situation that causes them anxiety. Instruct them to pay attention, as they are thinking, to the physical symptoms of their anxiety and to jot down notes.

4. While they are reflecting, draw a large outline of a person on the dry-erase board.

5. After the reflection period, let each teen label up to five of their most common physical anxiety symptoms on the outline you drew. They can color in an area, circle it, or even write their name on it.

6. Discuss what the board looks like.

DISCUSSION QUESTIONS

▶ In what areas of the body do you feel the most anxiety?

▶ What similarities did you notice with everyone in the group?

▶ What are the benefits of understanding the physical symptoms of anxiety in your body?

PRO TIPS

▶ Reassure the teens that there are no right or wrong answers—everyone experiences anxiety differently.

▶ Consider adding descriptions to each area labeled on the dry-erase board. For example, if someone circles the mouth, they would write "jaws clenched" next to it.

▶ If a dry-erase board is not available, teens can draw their own outlines on a piece of paper and note where they feel anxiety.

Anxiety Headlines

Examining how current events and news headlines can cause anxiety

Level 1
Understanding Anxiety

What You'll Need: Pencils and paper; dry-erase board and markers

Duration: 20 to 25 minutes

Best for: 2 to 6 people

LEADING THE ACTIVITY

1. Discuss how local and world events can play a role in a person's anxiety.

2. Have teens share where they get their news (e.g., television, social media, news feeds). Discuss whether these are reliable sources.

3. Have teens come up with three anxiety-causing headlines (either real or imagined) and write them on a piece of paper.

4. Ask each teen to choose one headline from the list to discuss with their peers.

5. Have them take turns writing their headlines on the board.

6. Discuss each headline, why it causes anxiety, and if there is anything the teen can do to prevent/reduce anxiety from reading this kind of headline in the future.

DISCUSSION QUESTIONS

▶ What types of headlines cause you the most anxiety?

▶ How can knowing the reliability of a news source help with your anxiety?

▶ What are some things you can do when struggling to make sense of local and worldwide events?

PRO TIPS

▶ Consider allowing teens to briefly explain the chosen headlines.

▶ Acknowledge that every headline, both big and small, has the potential to cause anxiety.

▶ Brainstorm a list of things teens can and can't control about current events unfolding around them.

Worry or Anxiety?

Defining and evaluating everyday worries to prevent them from feeding anxiety

Level 2
How Anxiety Affects Me

What You'll Need: Pencil and paper

Duration: 15 to 25 minutes

Best for: 1 person

LEADING THE ACTIVITY

1. Have the teen define worries and anxiety.

2. Ask them to come up with examples of worries. Discuss how worries are normal but can lead to anxiety.

3. Give the teen a few minutes to reflect on their everyday worries and then list up to 10.

4. Next have them rate these worries on a scale of 1 to 10 (with 10 causing the most anxiety).

5. Review the worry ratings and discuss whether these worries are a normal part of the teen's life or something that may be keeping them from enjoying life.

6. Discuss how they can deal with more intense worries to feel more at ease.

7. Next to each worry, have the teen write a specific way to cope with it using positive self-talk or coping strategies.

DISCUSSION QUESTIONS

▶ Which worries do you experience most frequently? Why do you think this happens?

▶ After talking about these worries, are there any ratings you would like to change?

▶ How can defining and evaluating your worries help reduce anxiety?

PRO TIPS

▶ Acknowledge that all worries are valid.

▶ Ask the teen to explain their reason for each rating.

▶ If time allows, have the teen identify which worries are about things they cannot control.

Anxiety Reflexes

Illustrating how anxious thoughts can lead to compulsive behaviors

Level 2
How Anxiety Affects Me

What You'll Need: Pencils and paper

Duration: 20 to 25 minutes

Best for: 2 to 8 people

LEADING THE ACTIVITY

1. Talk about **compulsive behaviors**, or actions done repeatedly when triggered by a specific thought or emotion.

2. Have the teens provide examples of how a thought can lead, almost like a reflex, to certain behaviors.

3. Discuss how anxious thoughts leading to compulsive behaviors. Mention how understanding this pattern can stop the cycle of negative thoughts and behaviors.

4. Give each teen a chance to illustrate a "mental reflex." Have the teen write an anxious thought on a piece of paper. As they read their thoughts, have them touch the piece of paper as if it were hot. As they take their hand away, have them say a compulsive behavior related to the thought.

5. Discuss the group's experience and follow up with an activity from Level 3 in this chapter to help teens find ways to reduce anxiety.

DISCUSSION QUESTIONS

▶ Discuss a time when anxious thoughts occurred very quickly—like pulling your hand from a hot pan.

▶ How does understanding that thoughts can trigger certain behaviors help you react to anxiety more productively?

PRO TIPS

▶ If you have a dry-erase board, write down the examples of anxious thoughts/compulsive behaviors as teens provide them. This can be a great visual aid.

▶ To make the activity more interesting, have one teen say an anxious thought while another teen names a compulsive behavior that may occur.

How Anxiety Affects Me

Understanding reactions to anxiety

Level 2
How Anxiety Affects Me

What You'll Need: Dice; dry-erase board and marker

Duration: 20 to 25 minutes

Best for: 3 to 6 people

LEADING THE ACTIVITY

1. Discuss how anxiety can impact different areas of our lives.

2. Write the following on the dry-erase board: *1. Thoughts, 2. Emotional, 3. Physical, 4. Behavioral, 5. Relationships, 6. Social Interactions.*

3. Have teens describe (in their own words) what each of these categories means.

4. Explain that each teen will get several turns to roll the dice and then explain how anxiety affects an area of their life based on the number they roll. For example, if they roll a 3, they would talk about physical reactions to anxiety, such as tension in the chest or shallow breathing.

5. Let each teen take several turns rolling the dice and discussing anxiety's effects.

6. Summarize and discuss the group's insights.

DISCUSSION QUESTIONS

▶ What were some of the typical reactions to anxiety mentioned?

▶ What are some answers that surprised you? Which did you relate to the most?

▶ How can understanding reactions to anxiety help you better manage it in the future?

PRO TIPS

▶ If no dice are available, write the categories on pieces of paper for teens to choose from.

▶ If a teen is having trouble with one of the categories, allow another teen to give input.

▶ Switch things around by providing a scenario, such as "worrying about grades," and then rolling the dice to play.

When Worries Get in the Way

Exploring how worries can keep us from going after something we really want

Level 2
How Anxiety Affects Me

What You'll Need: Paper; pencils; tape

Duration: 20 to 30 minutes

Best for: 2 to 6 people

LEADING THE ACTIVITY

1. Discuss how little worries that go unaddressed feed anxiety, which can keep people from accomplishing goals and moving forward in life.

2. Have the teens give examples of little worries that may turn into anxiety.

3. Divide them into pairs and explain that each pair will make a paper tower to symbolize worries that prevent them from achieving personal goals.

4. Assign each pair a source of anxiety based on the brainstorming results. Then give the following instructions:

   - Create the base of the tower using five to seven cylindrical shapes.

   - On each cylinder, write little worries associated with anxiety.

   - Place a flat piece of paper over the base and put three cylinders on top of it. On these three cylinders, write symptoms of anxiety or behaviors caused by the worries below.

   - Place another piece of paper over the second level. Then make one more cylinder that represents a decision you must make about your anxiety.

5. Have each pair explain their tower and what they learned while creating it.

DISCUSSION QUESTIONS

▶ Which of your small worries tend to build up over time?

▶ What challenges did you face while constructing the tower?

▶ How can managing small worries as they arise make it easier to achieve your personal goals?

PRO TIPS

▶ To make this activity easier, use empty toilet paper rolls for the cylinders.

▶ Add more levels to the tower for an extra challenge.

Anxiety Board Game

Creating a board game
to talk about worries

What You'll Need: Poster board; markers; pencils; dice;
simple objects to use as game pieces

Level 2
How Anxiety Affects Me

Duration: 20 to 40 minutes

Best for: 2 to 10 people

LEADING THE ACTIVITY

1. Divide the teens into small groups. Ask them to create a board game highlighting
   positive and negative ways to cope with anxiety. Explain that:

   - The game should have a path of 15 to 20 squares from start to finish.

   - Half of the squares should have positive numbers (1 to 3) and contain a
     positive self-talk or coping strategy.

   - The other half should have negative numbers (–1 to –3) and contain a negative
     coping strategy.

2. Have the teams swap completed boards and play the game, following these rules:

   - In turn, each player selects a game piece and rolls the dice, moving to the
     appropriate square.

   - The player discusses what is written on the square and why it will cause
     them forward or backward progress.

   - The teen then moves the determined number of spaces.

   - The first player to make it to the end of the path wins.

DISCUSSION QUESTIONS

▶ Describe what it felt like to make your board game. How did it make you think
   about anxiety?

▶ What interesting squares did you notice on your peers' game boards?

PRO TIPS

▶ Create other types of squares, like "lose a turn" or "double the dice roll," to make the
   game more fun. Make sure they add relevant anxiety reactions to these squares.

▶ Divide this activity into two sessions: creating the game and playing the other
   teams' game boards.

Mountain Meditation

Using guided meditation to see past anxious thoughts

What You'll Need: No materials needed

Duration: 15 to 20 minutes

Best for: 1 to 5 people

Level 3
Ways to Cope with Anxiety

LEADING THE ACTIVITY

1. Discuss how anxiety simply passes through us like other thoughts or emotions. While it may be uncomfortable in the moment, it eventually subsides.

2. With teen(s) seated or standing in a comfortable position and their eyes closed, guide them through the following meditation:

   - You are a mountain: tall, strong, and grounded.

   - It's springtime. With spring comes storms. The storms are strong, but they eventually pass, just like your anxious thoughts.

   - Now comes summer. The heat feels uncomfortable, but your inner core remains cool and collected.

   - Autumn brings changes. The leaves on your trees turn beautiful colors. You may be anxious about these changes, but you stand tall.

   - Winter brings cold and darkness. But even during the coldest nights, you stand strong. You know it will pass.

   - As the seasons pass, things change all around you, but your strength keeps you grounded, capable of managing whatever comes your way. You are a mountain. You are strong.

3. Allow teens to take a few deep breaths and reorient to the room.

DISCUSSION QUESTIONS

▶ Did this exercise help change your perspective of your anxiety? How?

▶ How can knowing that anxiety is temporary help you remain strong in difficult times?

PRO TIPS

▶ Try to eliminate any distractions during this exercise.

▶ Take long, meaningful pauses for quiet reflection after each prompt.

Talking Back to Fears

Brainstorming positive
ways to talk back to fears

Level 3
Ways to Cope with Anxiety

What You'll Need: Open area

Duration: 20 to 25 minutes

Best for: 4 to 10 people

LEADING THE ACTIVITY

1. Brainstorm thoughts and situations that cause anxiety.

2. Discuss how talking back to these fears using positive self-talk or coping strategies can help reduce anxiety.

3. Have the group stand in a line on one side of the room. Ask one teen to stand about 10 feet in front of the others and share an anxiety-inducing thought or situation.

4. Have the other teens each suggest some positive self-talk or coping strategies, and ask the teen in front to choose their favorite and second-favorite suggestions.

5. The teen with the favorite answer moves three steps forward. The teen with the second-favorite answer moves one step forward.

6. The teen in the front continues sharing anxiety-inducing thoughts and situations until one of the teens in the line catches up.

7. Give the winning teen an opportunity to stand in front of the others and repeat the activity.

8. Discuss ideas and insights gained during the session.

DISCUSSION QUESTIONS

▶ What were some key insights you took away from this activity?

▶ How can learning how to talk back to fears help you manage your anxiety?

PRO TIPS

▶ Provide a list of anxiety-inducing thoughts or situations for teens struggling to come up with their own.

▶ Remind teens that "the best" answer is subjective and up to the person in front.

▶ Discuss why the answer was considered the best.

Respond . . . Don't React

Responding, not reacting, to anxiety

Level 3
Ways to Cope with Anxiety

What You'll Need: Open area; cones or other items to mark spaces

Duration: 20 to 25 minutes

Best for: 4 to 8 people

LEADING THE ACTIVITY

1. Discuss how anxiety can cause the mind to race, making it difficult to think clearly. Explain that pausing for a few minutes helps us respond to anxiety instead of just reacting.

2. Clear the room of any potential tripping hazards. Set up two cones 10 to 15 feet apart. Have the group stand about 5 feet from the cones.

3. Pick a volunteer and ask them to choose an anxiety-inducing thought or situation.

4. Have the volunteer jog from one cone to the other, reciting the thought or situation aloud. In the meantime, ask the others to think of positive ways the jogger can respond to the thought or situation.

5. When someone has an answer, have them yell out: "Stop . . . breathe . . . breathe." Tell the jogger to stop and take deep breaths.

6. Have the teen with the idea share their positive response to the jogger's anxious thought and ask the jogger for feedback.

7. If the jogger likes the answer, have the person with the advice become the jogger. If not, repeat until the original jogger approves someone's advice.

DISCUSSION QUESTIONS

▶ How does your anxiety sometimes make it hard to think rationally?

▶ How can pausing, reflecting, and responding help you manage your anxiety?

PRO TIPS

▶ If someone's advice doesn't resonate with the jogger, have the jogger explain why before they continue running.

▶ Try other movements like dribbling a ball or keeping a balloon in the air while walking to make the activity more engaging.

My Safe Place

Combining quiet reflection and journaling to develop a safe place

Level 3
Ways to Cope with Anxiety

What You'll Need: Pencils and paper

Duration: 20 to 25 minutes

Best for: 1 to 4 people

LEADING THE ACTIVITY

1. Discuss how anxiety can cause us to feel uncomfortable and unsafe.

2. Explain that this activity is designed to help participants create a mental and physical safe place.

3. Give the teen(s) a few minutes to imagine an ideal safe place.

4. As they reflect, prompt them to visualize this place as vividly as possible. For example, "What do you see around you? Is there music or nature sounds?"

5. Have them journal about what they imagined, including as many details as possible.

6. Then ask them to list three things they can do to create a safe physical space—for example, make sure there's access to soothing music.

7. Encourage the teen(s) to share details about their safe space if they're comfortable.

8. Discuss how returning to the mental image of their safe space during anxious times can have a calming effect.

DISCUSSION QUESTIONS

▶ What do you like best about your safe space?

▶ How can you create a safe space in real life?

▶ Do you think revisiting the mental image of your safe place can help reduce anxiety? How?

PRO TIPS

▶ Encourage the teen(s) to come up with as many details as possible while visualizing.

▶ Those who don't want to journal can draw a picture of their safe space instead.

▶ Let the teen(s) choose which, if any, details to share about their safe spaces.

Anxiety Coping Plan

Brainstorming concrete
ways to manage anxieties

What You'll Need: Pencils and paper

Duration: 20 to 25 minutes

Level 3
Ways to Cope with Anxiety

Best for: 1 to 4 people

LEADING THE ACTIVITY

1. Discuss how having a concrete plan in anxious situations can make it easier to make good choices.

2. Explain that a good coping plan involves realistic ways to handle anxiety.

3. At the top of a piece of paper, ask the teen(s) to list at least five people, places, or things that trigger anxiety.

4. Below their anxiety triggers, have the teen(s) list at least three general coping strategies they've found helpful for managing anxiety.

5. On the opposite side of the paper, ask them to create their coping plan. Tell them to include at least five "I" statements naming their anxiety and stating how they plan to deal with it. For example, "When I am feeling alone and anxious, I will call my best friend and talk about my day."

6. Discuss progress and insights during this activity.

DISCUSSION QUESTIONS

▶ Describe a time when you felt anxious and weren't sure what to do.

▶ Why is it important to have specific coping strategies for your anxiety?

▶ How has creating this coping plan helped you put your anxiety into perspective?

PRO TIPS

▶ This is a highly individualized activity, so it works better with fewer participants. It's also more effective with teens who have previously participated in anxiety-related activities.

▶ Make sure teen(s) provide specific, realistic coping strategies for each "I" statement.

▶ Add a rewards clause at the end when the teen abides by the contract. For example, "When I use the coping strategies I listed, I can treat myself by …"

CHAPTER 7

DEPRESSION

Depression is a mood disorder characterized by intense and/or persistent feeling of sadness. While everyone experiences sadness as part of the human experience, depression can be unrelenting and affect everyday functioning.

Teens struggling with depression aren't simply feeling down or unwilling to "snap out of it." Depression is a serious mental health condition that often requires long-term treatment, including medication and counseling. The experiential activities in this chapter are designed to augment psychological counseling, not replace it. They provide opportunities for teens to understand their depression and develop coping skills.

This chapter has three types of activities: Quick Mood Boosters (Level 1) helps teens shift their mood and mind-set; Understanding Depression (Level 2) helps teens become aware of how depression affects their lives and ways to counteract these effects; and Managing Depression in Everyday Life (Level 3) gives practical tips and advice to manage the thoughts, emotions, and physical symptoms of depression.

We Are Connected

Feeling more connected to others

Level 1
Quick Mood Boosters

What You'll Need: Ball

Duration: 15 to 20 minutes

Best for: 4 to 10 people

LEADING THE ACTIVITY

1. Discuss how the more we get to know others, the more we find what we have in common. Being connected reduces feelings of isolation.

2. Have the group stand in a circle at least two shoulder widths apart.

3. Give the ball to one teen and have them say something about their favorite hobby, such as "I love tennis."

4. Have the teen throw the ball to another teen.

5. Ask that person to catch the ball and say something related to the first statement. For example, "I like tennis, too, but I like baseball better."

6. Continue the activity as time allows.

DISCUSSION QUESTIONS

▶ What have you learned about other people in the group today?

▶ Name a new connection you made during this activity.

▶ How can discovering you have more in common with your peers help you manage depression?

PRO TIPS

▶ If a teen can't find anything in common with the previous statement, they can simply acknowledge the statement and add their own. For example, "I never really tried painting, but I do like to spend time in nature."

▶ Encourage teens to expand on the previous statement. For example, "I like playing video games, too. Actually, my favorite type of video game is . . ."

▶ To lengthen the game, introduce other topics such as favorite foods or childhood memories.

Get Moving . . . Feel Better

Helping depression
through exercise

Level 1
Quick Mood Boosters

What You'll Need: Open area

Duration: 15 to 20 minutes

Best for: 3 to 8 people

LEADING THE ACTIVITY

1. Discuss how exercise can help with depression by venting negative emotions, releasing pleasure chemicals in the brain, and improving self-confidence.

2. Have the group stand at least four shoulder lengths apart and get comfortable.

3. Tell them they are about to participate in a short, low-impact exercise routine.

4. Ask them to follow these steps:

   - Walk in place for 30 seconds.

   - Stand tall and stretch your arms to the ceiling. Take five deep breaths.

   - Do jumping jacks for 30 seconds.

   - Stand tall, put your hands above your head, and lean to the right side. Hold for 25 seconds. Repeat on the other side.

   - March in place for 30 seconds.

   - Stand on your left foot for 45 seconds. Switch sides.

   - Jog in place for 30 seconds.

   - Stand tall, take five deep breaths, and feel your whole body relax.

5. Explain how this routine combines elements of cardio activities and yoga—both effective ways to boost our mood.

DISCUSSION QUESTIONS

- What exercise did you like the most? The least?

- Describe how you felt after the routine.

- How can incorporating even short periods of exercise help improve your mood?

PRO TIPS

- Adjust exercises and duration based on your group's ability level.

- You don't have to say how long they should do each exercise—this might distract teens.

Do the Venting Dance

Venting feelings
using dance

Level 1
Quick Mood Boosters

What You'll Need: Open area

Duration: 15 to 20 minutes

Best for: 4 to 10 people

LEADING THE ACTIVITY

1. Discuss how simple movements, like stomping your feet, can help express or vent feelings. Brainstorm other ways to vent frustration through movement.

2. Call out an emotion that often needs to be vented, such as frustration.

3. Have each person in the group create a movement to vent this emotion.

4. Now, have the group work together to combine their movements into a dance routine.

5. Repeat steps 2 through 4 with other emotions as time allows.

6. Discuss how this activity felt.

DISCUSSION QUESTIONS

▶ Which movements in this routine did you enjoy the most?

▶ How did you feel while performing the dance routines?

▶ How can using movements like dance help vent intense feelings?

PRO TIPS

▶ Some teens may be reluctant to do movements in front of a group. Give them an alternative, like saying a phrase, that can still be incorporated into a routine.

▶ If possible, incorporate music into the dance routine to make it more engaging.

▶ Try to incorporate two contrasting sets of emotions into a routine—for example, bored and excited—to explore how different emotions look side by side.

Whole Body Smile

Visualizing changing moods and developing gratitude

Level 1
Quick Mood Boosters

What You'll Need: No materials needed

Duration: 15 to 20 minutes

Best for: 1 to 5 people

LEADING THE ACTIVITY

1. Tell the teen(s) they will be participating in a short visualization exercise based on the simple act of smiling.

2. Provide the following instructions:

   - Take a few deep breaths and close your eyes (if comfortable).

   - Picture something that makes you happy, like a favorite person, possession, or fond memory.

   - Imagine yourself smiling at this happy thought. You may find yourself actually starting to smile. How does it feel to smile?

   - Imagine that smile spreading throughout your body, starting with your head, then down your neck, and so on, until your whole body is smiling one big smile.

   - With your whole body smiling, extend your smile to all the things that make you happy and hold it for a few moments.

   - Now return your attention to your breath. When ready, open your eyes.

DISCUSSION QUESTIONS

▶ How did you feel during this exercise?

▶ What changes did you notice in your thoughts and mood after this exercise?

▶ How can short exercises like this break the cycle of negative thoughts and emotions?

PRO TIPS

▶ Add pauses between each step to help the teen(s) process.

▶ If a teen laughs or becomes uncomfortable during this exercise, let them open their eyes and sit quietly while others finish.

Filling My Happy Space

Brainstorming and illustrating ways to add more happiness to our lives

What You'll Need: Pencils and paper; markers or colored pencils; old magazines or access to other appropriate images

Duration: 20 to 30 minutes

Best for: 1 to 5 people

Level 1
Quick Mood Boosters

LEADING THE ACTIVITY

1. Discuss how being surrounded by things, people, and activities that make us happy can help counteract the effects of depression.
2. Allow the teen(s) a few minutes to quietly reflect on things that make them happy.
3. Ask them to imagine a room filled with these things.
4. Give them about 10 minutes to make an illustration of their happy places.
5. Have them share their happy space and explain what they filled it with.

DISCUSSION QUESTIONS

▶ What are some of your favorite things in your happy space?

▶ What were some great ideas others had for their happy space?

▶ How can having access to the things that make you happy help ease the symptoms of depression?

PRO TIPS

▶ Encourage teen(s) to think about more than just possessions—for example, pets, playing cards with a friend, or a beautiful nature scene.

▶ Allow them to get creative and complete their artwork in any way they wish—for example, words representing happy things or a collage.

▶ Consider asking what they already have in their happy place drawing and things that they wish they had.

Blindfolded Self-Portrait

Practicing
self-acceptance

Level 2
Understanding Depression

What You'll Need: Blindfolds or something else to cover the eyes; pencils and paper

Duration: 15 to 20 minutes

Best for: 1 to 6 people

LEADING THE ACTIVITY

1. Have the teen(s) define **self-portrait** and the information this genre of art often conveys about the subject, such as personality and physical attributes.

2. Tell them they will have 5 minutes to create their self-portrait while blindfolded. Discuss the challenges this may present.

3. Explain that the self-portrait can include leisure interests, positive qualities, and any other information they wish to share.

4. After completing their self-portrait, ask them to take off the blindfold to look at and share their work.

5. Have them discuss how they feel about their self-portrait and how the blindfold made this activity difficult. Talk about how adversity can get in the way of creating an ideal life.

6. Discuss how self-acceptance, especially during difficult times, can help ease negative feelings about ourselves.

DISCUSSION QUESTIONS

▶ Did your portrait turn out different than you expected? In what way?

▶ Talk about a time when obstacles got in the way of your plans.

▶ How can self-acceptance help you adapt to life, especially in times of adversity?

PRO TIPS

▶ If the teen(s) don't want to be blindfolded, find other ways to obscure their view.

▶ Before drawing, teen(s) can brainstorm their positive qualities to help them focus.

▶ Since many portraits will not come out the way the individual intended, ensure that the group remains respectful and supportive while sharing portraits.

Walk Away Your Thoughts

Using walking to break negative thought patterns

Level 2
Understanding Depression

What You'll Need: No materials needed

Duration: 15 to 20 minutes

Best for: 1 to 6 people

Prep: Locate an indoor or outdoor area large enough for teens to walk around.

LEADING THE ACTIVITY

1. Discuss how people with depression can get stuck in a cycle of ruminating thoughts. Explain that simple activities, like going for a walk, can help break the cycle.

2. Give the teen(s) 5 to 10 minutes to simply walk around and notice what is around them. Ask them to mentally recite the things they see while walking whenever they find themselves challenged with a negative thought or emotion.

3. After the walk, allow the teens to discuss their thoughts and feelings about the activity.

DISCUSSION QUESTIONS

▶ How did you feel during the walk?

▶ Describe a time when you had trouble releasing negative thoughts or emotions.

▶ How can you incorporate walking into your daily life to help refocus your thoughts?

PRO TIPS

▶ Provide a list of things the teen(s) can look for while walking to help them focus.

▶ If indoors, place interesting objects around the room for them to name while walking.

▶ Encourage the teen(s) not to socialize during this activity, since it's easier to simulate rumination when walking alone.

My Community, My Resources

Mapping local resources
for help with depression

What You'll Need: Paper; pencils; colored pencils; markers

Duration: 20 to 30 minutes

Level 2
Understanding Depression

Best for: 1 to 5 people

LEADING THE ACTIVITY

1. Discuss times when the teen(s) felt depressed and alone.

2. Brainstorm resources they can use when struggling with depression.

3. Give teen(s) a few minutes to think about people or places they can go to when feeling overwhelmed with depression. If necessary, give prompts, such as "Who do you trust when you need to talk about your emotions?"

4. Have them create a "roadmap" to identify safe, trusted people and places that can help them manage their depression.

5. Encourage them to put as many safe landmarks as possible on the map and list why each is helpful. For example, "A trip to a local park can help me feel less isolated."

6. Share and discuss the maps.

DISCUSSION QUESTIONS

▶ What are some of your most trusted resources when feeling depressed? Why?

▶ What are some landmarks you can easily visit when feeling depressed?

▶ How can having a list of resources make you more willing to reach out for help?

PRO TIPS

▶ Use ideas from the initial brainstorming process to help the teen(s) identify landmarks.

▶ Let them color-code their landmarks. For example, orange could be places that make them feel happy, and blue could be people that help them calm down.

▶ If they have difficulty creating a map, they can write "If . . . then . . ." statements instead. For example, "If I feel overwhelmed with my family situation, then I can talk to my best friend for support."

Roll with Gratitude

Cultivating gratitude

Level 2
Understanding Depression

What You'll Need: Dice; dry-erase board and markers; list of gratitude categories

Duration: 15 to 25 minutes

Best for: 3 to 8 people

Prep: Create a list of categories teens can be grateful for, such as health, family, special talents, or friendships, and write them on the dry-erase board.

LEADING THE ACTIVITY

1. Have the group define gratitude and give examples of things they're grateful for. Explain that feeling gratitude can ease depression symptoms by helping us focus on more positive aspects of life.

2. Have teens sit around a table. Explain the rules of the "gratitude game":

   - In turn, each player rolls a die and lists things they're grateful for based on the number rolled. For example, if you roll a 5, you list five things.

   - Players choose the things they're grateful for from the categories listed on the board.

   - Each player selects a different category from the list.

DISCUSSION QUESTIONS

▶ In which category was it most difficult to find things you were grateful for? Why?

▶ What are some answers that surprised you or made you think?

▶ How can taking time each day for gratitude help change your outlook on life?

PRO TIPS

▶ If teens have trouble with a category, they can list general things they're grateful for.

▶ Provide a stack of cards with different categories; then have teens pick a random card before each roll.

▶ To make the game more challenging, have teens come up with their own categories for each round.

Quick Connections

Feeling more connected
to peers

Level 2
Understanding Depression

What You'll Need: Ping-pong or high-bounce balls

Duration: 20 to 30 minutes

Best for: 4 to 12 people (even-numbered groups preferred)

Prep: Number the balls in pairs (two number 1's, two number 2's, etc.) and ensure that there are enough for all participants.

LEADING THE ACTIVITY

1. Have the group line up on one side of the room. Throw all of the balls toward the other side of the room.

2. Instruct each teen to grab one ball.

3. Once everyone has a ball, tell them to pair up based on their ball's number.

4. Instruct each pair to spend 1 to 2 minutes discovering three things about their partner.

5. Have each pair discuss what they have in common.

6. Repeat the process so different teens have a chance to pair up.

7. Discuss the group's experience.

DISCUSSION QUESTIONS

▶ Name something you learned about another person today.

▶ How did it feel to discover similarities with your peers?

▶ How can making connections with others make people with depression feel less isolated?

PRO TIPS

▶ If no balls are available, you can use playing cards or numbered cards.

▶ For each round, provide a different category to discuss.

▶ Increase the number of similarities each team must come up with to make the game more challenging.

Starting the Conversation

Practicing talking about issues with someone you trust

Level 3
Managing Depression in Everyday Life

What You'll Need: Note cards

Duration: 20 to 25 minutes

Best for: 2 to 8 people

LEADING THE ACTIVITY

1. Discuss how talking about difficult feelings with a trusted person can help those struggling with depression. Ask teens to provide examples.

2. Give two note cards to each person. On one card, have them write down a topic they find difficult to talk about. On the other, have them write down a description of a trusted person they'd feel comfortable confiding in (e.g., basketball coach or best friend). Assure them that their answers will remain anonymous. Collect both sets of cards and shuffle them.

3. Have the teens pair up. Ask one member of each pair to select a card from each pile.

4. Give the pairs a few minutes to role-play based on the topic/person card combination they picked.

5. Discuss the group's progress and findings.

DISCUSSION QUESTIONS

▶ How hard is it for you to reach out when you are feeling depressed? Why?

▶ During the role-play, how did your partner reach out to others for support?

▶ How can having a support system of trusted individuals help you manage depression?

PRO TIPS

▶ Encourage teens to make the role-playing as realistic as possible by adding details to their conversations.

▶ This activity is best for groups of teens who already have some rapport.

▶ Pause the role-plays to highlight positive examples of reaching out to others—for example, asking if they have a few minutes to talk; going to talk in a safe, private location; or saying they feel like they need extra support at the moment.

My Free Time Schedule

Evaluating how teens
use their free time

Level 3
Managing Depression
in Everyday Life

What You'll Need: Dry-erase board and markers; pencils;
paper; highlighters; colored pencils or markers

Duration: 25 to 35 minutes

Best for: 1 to 6 people

LEADING THE ACTIVITY

1. Discuss how the leisure activities we participate in during our free time can have
   a major impact on our physical and mental health—including depression.

2. Have the teen(s) provide examples of leisure activities to ensure that they understand the concept. Brainstorm categories, such as physical activity and screen
   time. Write them on the dry-erase board.

3. Ask them to reflect on the previous weekend, create an hour-by-hour recap of
   what they did during their waking hours, and color code the activities by category.

4. Encourage them to share their recaps.

5. Discuss how leisure activities help us achieve balance and overall well-being.

6. Have them create a leisure schedule for the next weekend, incorporating a variety
   of categories.

DISCUSSION QUESTIONS

▶ What are your favorite ways to spend your free time?

▶ Which activities do you think are most helpful for managing depression?

▶ How ready and willing are you to stick to your new leisure schedule?
   Why or why not?

PRO TIPS

▶ Intervene if teens judge another teen's recap, especially if they are struggling
   with depression.

▶ After the category brainstorming session, select specific categories you want to
   see highlighted in the teen's schedule. For example, physical, social, creative, and
   relaxing activities.

Self-Care Brainstorm

Exploring self-care
strategies to ease
depression

Level 3
Managing Depression
in Everyday Life

What You'll Need: Pencils and paper

Duration: 20 to 25 minutes

Best for: 1 to 4 people

LEADING THE ACTIVITY

1. Define **self-care** as activities people do intentionally to care for their mental, emotional, and physical well-being. Have the teen(s) provide examples. Explain that there are many ways to provide self-care.

2. Introduce these six categories: physical, psychological, professional/educational, personal, spiritual, and emotional. Ask the teens(s) to define and give examples for each category.

3. Have them divide a piece of paper into six sections, one for each category.

4. Give them 1 to 2 minutes to brainstorm and jot down self-care ideas for each category.

5. Then ask them to place stars next to the self-care ideas that resonate best with them.

6. Share self-care ideas and discuss.

DISCUSSION QUESTIONS

▶ What were some of your favorite self-care ideas?

▶ For which categories did you find it the hardest to come up with ideas?

▶ How do you feel self-care can help manage depression?

PRO TIPS

▶ For larger groups, hang poster boards with each category around the room. Have the teen(s) rotate to each station to fill in ideas.

▶ Make sure they understand the different categories before brainstorming.

▶ If necessary, have them go through their results and talk about positive self-care and how it can help lessen symptoms of depression.

Obstacle Course

Engaging in simple physical exercise ideas to help with depression

Level 3
Managing Depression in Everyday Life

What You'll Need: Paper; tape

Duration: 20 to 30 minutes

Best for: 4 to 10 people

Prep: Locate an indoor or outdoor area large enough for teens to exercise in.

LEADING THE ACTIVITY

1. Ask the group to discuss their favorite physical activities and how they feel after engaging in them.

2. Explain that physical activity can help reduce the symptoms of depression by releasing pleasure chemicals in the brain and lowering stress.

3. Ask each teen to demonstrate a physical activity that helps them feel better to the group.

4. Create an obstacle course/relay race incorporating all of the physical activities mentioned. Set up stations around the exercise area with written instructions. Tape the explanations to the wall or secure them on the ground.

5. Divide the group into teams.

6. Have one person on each team complete the course and then tag another team member to go next.

7. Continue until everyone finishes the course.

DISCUSSION QUESTIONS

▶ Which physical activities did you enjoy? Which were the most challenging?

▶ Name one way you can incorporate more physical activity into your daily life to help with depression.

PRO TIPS

▶ If teens come up with physical activities that require equipment you don't have, they can act out the physical activity.

▶ Feel free to include other stations not mentioned, such as a simple yoga pose.

▶ Ensure that the activities are within everyone's capability.

Using My Talents

Identifying the benefits of reaching out to others

Level 3
Managing Depression
in Everyday Life

What You'll Need: Paper; pencils; colored pencils or markers

Duration: 20 to 30 minutes

Best for: 1 to 6 people

LEADING THE ACTIVITY

1. Discuss how helping others can help boost confidence and self-worth and improve symptoms of depression.

2. Talk about how teens can use their unique talents to help others.

3. Give the teen(s) 5 to 10 minutes to make an advertisement highlighting their unique talents. If necessary, give a few examples of talents. The teen(s) will share the ads and explain how their talents could be useful to others.

4. Discuss different volunteer ideas and opportunities such as tutoring or helping at a food pantry.

5. On the back of the ad, have the teen(s) list three concrete ways they can help others.

6. Give them an opportunity to share how they intend to help others.

DISCUSSION QUESTIONS

▶ Which of your talents do you think will be most useful for helping others?

▶ How do you feel about reaching out to help others?

▶ How do you think selfless actions like helping others can help manage depression?

PRO TIPS

▶ Give prompts for the advertisement, such as "My name is . . . and here is how I can help."

▶ Provide a list of volunteer opportunities in the community teens can explore.

▶ Help teen(s) create three actionable steps to start helping others based on their list—for example, check my schedule for availability, call the volunteer coordinator, or participate in a volunteer orientation.

CHAPTER 8

BULLYING

Bullying refers to unwanted aggressive behavior that is usually directed at someone the bully perceives as vulnerable. It can occur in person or online and includes behaviors like harassment, name-calling, stalking, intimidation, and physical aggression. Unfortunately, many teens don't have the coping and communication skills to handle bullying on their own.

At this stage of development, teens are especially vulnerable to bullying because they often seek the approval and acceptance of their peers. A bully can undermine all that a teen has worked for to establish a sense of belonging and self-esteem. The activities in this chapter allow a teen to identify what bullying is and how to reduce and/or eliminate its harmful effects.

The activities in this chapter are divided into three levels: Understanding Bullying (Level 1), Dealing with Bullies (Level 2), and Becoming Bully-Proof (Level 3). Level 1 activities allow teens to understand bullying behavior and what it looks like. Level 2 activities give teens practical approaches to handling bullies. Finally, Level 3 activities address steps teens can take to keep from being bullied.

What Is a Bully?

Taking a closer look at teens' perceptions of bullying

Level 1
Understanding Bullying

What You'll Need: Pencils; paper; dry-erase board and markers

Duration: 20 to 25 minutes

Best for: 2 to 8 people

LEADING THE ACTIVITY

1. Ask the teens to give their personal definitions of a bully.

2. Discuss behavior common to bullies.

3. Give the teens 7 to 10 minutes to create a profile of a bully, similar to a "Wanted" poster. It should list typical bullying behaviors, whom the bully interacts with, whom the bully targets, and what may be motivating the bully.

4. Give the teens a chance to present their bully profiles.

5. Discuss the findings.

DISCUSSION QUESTIONS

▶ What were the most common characteristics of a bully?

▶ How was your bully profile different from those of others?

▶ How can identifying bullying behaviors help prevent you from being a target?

PRO TIPS

▶ Teens do not have to think of a specific person, just create a profile based on their experience and knowledge of bullying.

▶ If time allows, ask them to create two profiles: a typical bully and a cyberbully.

▶ To help teens understand different types of bullying, spend extra time discussing a range of bullying behaviors in different contexts.

Types of Bullying

Discussing and evaluating different types of bullying

Level 1
Understanding Bullying

What You'll Need: Pencils; paper; dry-erase board and markers

Duration: 20 to 25 minutes

Best for: 2 to 8 people

LEADING THE ACTIVITY

1. Ask the group to describe the type of bullying they're most familiar with.

2. Discuss how bullying comes in many forms. Brainstorm types of bullying and list them on one side of the dry-erase board.

3. Add any of the following types not mentioned by the group: cyberbullying, hazing, harassment, teasing, creating conflict, name-calling, isolating a person, spreading rumors, threatening, practical jokes, terrorizing, hate speech, hitting, and intimidation.

4. Have the teens write down on a piece of paper the five types of bullying listed on the board that they consider the most harmful.

5. Then read out each type of bullying on the board and ask the teens to raise their hand if it's on their top-five list. Keep a tally next to each type of bullying.

6. Discuss the findings of the group.

DISCUSSION QUESTIONS

▶ What is the most common form of bullying you have encountered or witnessed?

▶ What types of bullying discussed during this activity surprised you? Why?

▶ How can understanding types of bullying make you more resilient to a bully's actions?

PRO TIPS

▶ If time allows, consider having teens role-play types of bullying to clarify how they differ.

▶ Discuss how all forms of bullying, even those considered minor, can have negative effects on others.

▶ Have each teen explain what they think is the most harmful form of bullying.

Bigger Than a Bully

Helping teens shift their perspectives on bullies

Level 1
Understanding Bullying

What You'll Need: Modeling clay or Play-Doh

Duration: 20 to 30 minutes

Best for: 1 to 6 people

LEADING THE ACTIVITY

1. Have the teen(s) think of a time when they encountered or witnessed bullying.

2. Ask them to recreate the scene using modeling clay or Play-Doh. Have them show how the bully perceived the teen and how the teen perceived the bully.

3. Reassure the teens that their sculptures don't need to be realistic; they should just symbolize the interaction.

4. Share and discuss the teens' creations.

5. Talk about how practicing confidence and projecting it through our posture can reduce the effects of bullying behavior. Provide examples of confident posture.

6. Instruct the teens to keep the bully clay figure the same but rework the target figure as more confident and resilient to the bully.

7. Discuss the results.

DISCUSSION QUESTIONS

▶ How did your first scene differ from your second one?

▶ What does confidence look like to you?

▶ What are some ways you can practice confident body language to deal with bullying behavior?

PRO TIPS

▶ If modeling clay is not available, teen(s) can draw or even act out a scene.

▶ Guide teen(s) while they're making their initial clay scene. For example, "How can you depict the body language of the bully and target?"

▶ Some types of bullying may be harder to depict. If teens struggle with a scene, suggest an easier common scene to work with.

Cyberbullying Screenshots

Understanding what
cyberbullying looks like

Understanding Bullying

What You'll Need: Pencils; paper; colored pencils or markers

Duration: 20 to 25 minutes

Best for: 1 to 6 people

LEADING THE ACTIVITY

1. Discuss different types of bullying. Have teen(s) provide examples.

2. Introduce cyberbullying—who does it, what it looks like, and so on.

3. Next, discuss cyberbullying's effects on people, such as making them feel exposed, vulnerable, humiliated, and dissatisfied.

4. Have teen(s) draw a "screenshot" that illustrates typical cyberbullying.

5. Allow each teen to present their screenshot and talk about why they believe it is bullying.

6. Talk about the group's findings.

DISCUSSION QUESTIONS

▶ What were some interesting examples of cyberbullying you saw today?

▶ How can cyberbullying be hurtful or damaging to an individual?

▶ How can understanding cyberbullying prevent you from being targeted in the future?

PRO TIPS

▶ Allow teen(s) to make additional screenshots if time allows.

▶ To help teen(s) understand its breadth, break down cyberbullying into different categories, like harassment, name-calling, hateful speech, and so on.

▶ If time allows, talk about how each screenshot may affect someone.

Hurtful Words

Identifying hurtful
remarks and discussing
how to ignore them

Level 1
Understanding Bullying

What You'll Need: Dry-erase board and markers

Duration: 20 to 25 minutes

Best for: 2 to 8 people

LEADING THE ACTIVITY

1. List some ways that bullies behave toward others.

2. Discuss how words can hurt. Have teens name hurtful words bullies may use and write them on the board.

3. Once there are several hurtful words on the board, talk about how these words can negatively affect us.

4. Discuss ways to ignore hurtful remarks, like avoiding the bully, walking away, reminding yourself the situation is not your fault, walking with a buddy, and so on.

5. Have the teens talk about ways they've dealt with someone using hurtful words in the past.

DISCUSSION QUESTIONS

▶ Why do you think words have such an impact on people?

▶ Talk about a time when you witnessed or encountered someone using hurtful words.

▶ How can learning to ignore hurtful words make you more resilient to them?

PRO TIPS

▶ Talk about why certain words are more hurtful than others.

▶ If time allows, have teens role-play ways to ignore or walk away from a bully's hurtful words.

▶ Set limits to which words can be used during this session.

Being Assertive

Practicing assertiveness through role-play

Level 2
Dealing with Bullies

What You'll Need: Dry-erase board and markers

Duration: 20 to 25 minutes

Best for: 4 to 8 people

LEADING THE ACTIVITY

1. Discuss characteristics that could make people easier targets for bullies. List them on the left side of the dry-erase board.

2. Brainstorm characteristics that could make people less likely to be a target of bullies. List them in the middle of the board.

3. Define **assertiveness** as appearing confident and bold in statements and actions. Have the teens give examples of assertive behavior.

4. If necessary, provide examples of assertiveness, such as speaking with confidence and calmly walking away from someone trying to provoke.

5. Brainstorm assertive responses teens can use with bullies. List them on the right side of the board.

6. Have them role-play scenarios where a bully may be trying to provoke them.

7. Discuss how they handled the role-plays.

DISCUSSION QUESTIONS

▶ What are some common traits of assertive behavior?

▶ Why do you think bullies back down when faced with assertiveness?

▶ How can practicing assertiveness help when you are being bullied or faced with other difficult circumstances?

PRO TIPS

▶ If a teen has trouble being assertive during a role-play, pause and ask for feedback from others in the group.

▶ Make sure teens understand the difference between assertive and aggressive behavior.

It's Not Your Fault

Realizing that bullying is not your fault and developing a more objective perspective about it

What You'll Need: Dry-erase board and markers

Duration: 20 to 30 minutes

Best for: 4 to 10 people

Level 2
Dealing with Bullies

LEADING THE ACTIVITY

1. Discuss some common ways teens are bullied and list them on the dry-erase board.

2. Choose one scenario and ask two volunteers to act it out. Give them a few minutes to plan their role-play.

3. Afterward, talk about why the person may have been targeted by the bully, what emotional and communication issues the bully may be dealing with, and any other circumstances that may lead to bullying.

4. Discuss some reasons the person being bullied is not at fault and write them on the board.

5. Continue role-plays and discussion periods as time allows.

6. Finish by summarizing the group's insights.

DISCUSSION QUESTIONS

▸ Why might the person being bullied think the bullying was their fault?

▸ Why should you consider what the bully may be going through?

▸ How does looking into the factors that cause bullying behavior help you understand that it's not the victim's fault?

PRO TIPS

▸ Make sure role-plays remain respectful to avoid triggering someone dealing with trauma or other issues.

▸ Try to provide opportunities for teens to see that a bully may be suffering as much as the target. Remind teens that bullying is never appropriate but that bullying behavior may be the result of not knowing how to properly communicate and express feelings.

▸ Reiterate that bullying is never the victim's fault.

Confident Posture

Practicing confident body language

Level 2
Dealing with Bullies

What You'll Need: Pencils and paper

Duration: 20 to 25 minutes

Best for: 1 to 6 people

LEADING THE ACTIVITY

1. Talk about body language and what it can communicate. Provide examples by assuming different postures. Have the teen(s) guess what each posture communicates.

2. Ask the teen(s) to draw a picture of someone whose posture displays a lack of confidence. Have them label key features.

3. Ask them to share to their drawings.

4. On the other side of the paper, have them draw someone who appears confident and label key features.

5. Ask them to compare the two drawings and share their findings.

6. Have each teen come to the front of the room, assume their most confident posture, and explain why their body language communicates confidence.

DISCUSSION QUESTIONS

▸ Do you feel your normal posture communicates confidence? Why or why not?

▸ Name someone you consider very confident. Why did you choose this person?

▸ How can being mindful of your body language make you appear more confident?

PRO TIPS

▸ If necessary, provide tips on confident body language after teen(s) share their pictures of a person lacking confidence.

▸ Give extra encouragement and guidance to shy and timid teen(s).

▸ If time allows, have everyone stand up and display a non-confident pose at the end of the activity. Then have them switch to a confident one.

It's Okay to Walk Away

Determining when it is
best to walk away

Level 2
Dealing with Bullies

What You'll Need: Pencils; paper; dry-erase board and markers

Duration: 25 to 30 minutes

Best for: 3 to 6 people

LEADING THE ACTIVITY

1. Ask the teens how they feel about simply walking away from bullying behaviors.

2. Discuss how walking away with confidence may be the best option to disengage the bully. It lets you maintain your composure while showing that you don't want to waste your time dealing with them. Talk about what it means to confidently walk away.

3. Give the teens 5 to 10 minutes to create a poem or rap about walking away from a bully. Prompt them with the title: "I'm Walking Away . . . and It's Okay."

4. Encourage them to use examples of being bullied, walking away confidently, and maintaining composure when faced with difficult emotions.

5. Allow them to share their poem or rap. Write some of the better lines or verses on the board for discussion.

DISCUSSION QUESTIONS

▶ Describe a time you walked away from a bully or other unpleasant situation. What happened afterward?

▶ Were there any lines from others' poems or raps that resonated with you?

▶ How can walking away be effective when dealing with bullies?

PRO TIPS

▶ Encourage the teens to get as creative as possible while constructing the poem or rap.

▶ Set ground rules, such as using appropriate language and being respectful.

▶ If teens are having trouble, provide them with one or two lines to get started.

Silent Mantras to Stay Strong

Staying strong in the face of bullies and other adversity

Level 2
Dealing with Bullies

What You'll Need: Dry-erase board and markers; note cards; pencils; colored pencils or markers

Duration: 25 to 35 minutes

Best for: 1 to 5 people

LEADING THE ACTIVITY

1. Discuss how bullies love to get in others' heads. Their words and actions are meant to break you down and take away your confidence.

2. Introduce the concept of **mantras**, short phrases one mentally repeats to help reorient thoughts.

3. Have the teen(s) sit comfortably and close their eyes. Ask them to focus on their breathing. With each exhale, have them mentally recite a mantra like "I am calm."

4. After 3 to 5 minutes, have them open their eyes and discuss how the exercise felt.

5. Explain that mantras can be an effective internal defense against bullying. Brainstorm different mantras to use for bullying. Write examples on the board.

6. Have them write down their mantras on a note card and decorate them if they wish. Suggest that they can carry their mantras around in their pocket or purse as a reminder. Encourage them to practice the mantras at least five times a day.

DISCUSSION QUESTIONS

▶ What differences did you notice after doing the exercise?

▶ How did you choose your mantra?

▶ How can reciting a mantra help replace negative feelings, especially when you're being bullied?

PRO TIPS

▶ Encourage the teen(s) to start their mantra with "I am . . ." to think about themselves in the moment rather than an idealized version of themselves.

▶ Provide additional examples of mantras, such as "I am strong" or "I am confident."

▶ Ask them to record how many times they practice their mantras each day.

Super-Me!

Celebrating and affirming
our positive attributes

Level 3
Becoming Bully-Proof

What You'll Need: Paper; pencils; colored pencils or markers

Duration: 25 to 35 minutes

Best for: 1 to 6 people

LEADING THE ACTIVITY

1. Discuss how teens tend to rely on others' feedback and comments for self-approval. Ask the teen(s) to give examples of when and where they get feedback, such as social media.

2. Have them discuss the positives and negatives of seeking others' approval for validation.

3. Discuss how being aware of our positive attributes and affirming them can make us less reliant on others' approval.

4. Ask them to create a list of their positive attributes starting with the phrase "I am." For example, "I am a great listener."

5. Have them create a personal superhero avatar, highlighting these positive attributes.

6. Allow them to share and explain their avatars.

7. Discuss the positive attributes mentioned.

DISCUSSION QUESTIONS

▶ What positive attributes are you most proud of?

▶ Describe a time when you allowed someone's comments to make you feel less confident.

▶ How can relying on your own judgment make you more resilient to other people's opinions and negative comments?

PRO TIPS

▶ If they are not into superheroes, have teen(s) create another type of avatar or use literary or historical figures they admire.

▶ Encourage them to come up with creative names and concepts for their avatar.

My Confidence Boosters

Feeling happier and
more confident through
leisure activities

Level 3
Becoming Bully-Proof

What You'll Need: Dry-erase board and markers; pencils; paper;
colored pencils or markers

Duration: 20 to 30 minutes

Best for: 2 to 8 people

LEADING THE ACTIVITY

1. Discuss how participating in enjoyable leisure activities can help us feel happier and more confident. Brainstorm a list of leisure activities that may improve confidence.

2. Have the teens pick their favorite leisure activities and create an advertisement for them.

3. Tell them the ads should mention how the activities help boost confidence and any other benefits they provide.

4. Give the teens a chance to share their work.

5. Discuss any insights gained about leisure activities and how the teens can include more activities in their everyday lives.

DISCUSSION QUESTIONS

▶ How does your chosen activity boost your confidence?

▶ What were some activities others mentioned that you would be interested in trying? Why?

▶ How can building confidence make you better able to deal with bullying?

PRO TIPS

▶ If necessary, spend some time talking about the potential benefits of positive leisure activities. Provide an example, like playing basketball, and brainstorm benefits it offers.

▶ Explain that leisure activities benefit people in different ways. There are no right or wrong answers.

▶ Consider hanging up these advertisements as a reminder of the importance of doing what you enjoy.

Safety in Numbers

Building a support
network to
prevent bullying

Level 3
Becoming Bully-Proof

What You'll Need: Soft ball or pieces of paper

Duration: 20 to 25 minutes

Best for: 4 to 9 people

LEADING THE ACTIVITY

1. Discuss how bullies like to isolate their targets to make them feel more vulnerable.

2. Choose two volunteers, with one teen as the bully and the other the target.

3. Have the "bully" throw a soft ball or a crumpled piece of paper at the "target." Discuss how one-on-one interactions make it easier for a bully to target someone.

4. Have another teen stand with the target. Allow the bully to throw the ball at the target again, but this time ask the third teen to try to deflect the ball.

5. Discuss how having people around makes it harder for a bully to target a person.

6. Finally, have the rest of the group stand around the target and try to deflect the ball when the bully throws it again.

7. Explain how support networks can reduce the effects of bullying and make a person less likely to be bullied. Talk about how teens can build these support networks to stand up to bullies.

DISCUSSION QUESTIONS

▷ Describe a time when a bully targeted you or someone you know.

▷ Why do you think a bully tries to isolate their targets?

▷ Why should you reach out to others when you feel you are being bullied?

PRO TIPS

▷ Ensure that the object being thrown is soft and won't cause any damage.

▷ Consider elaborating the scenario with the first teen role-playing the bully's words and posture and the second acting out the target's response.

▷ Encourage teens to create actionable steps to prevent themselves from being isolated by a bully.

Staying Safe Online

Preventing cyberbullying and staying safe online

Level 3
Becoming Bully-Proof

What You'll Need: Dry-erase board and markers

Duration: 20 to 30 minutes

Best for: 2 to 8 people

LEADING THE ACTIVITY

1. Discuss how the internet and technology have given bullies new ways to victimize others.

2. Talk about different types of cyberbullying and write down specific examples on the board.

3. Guide teens to come up with solutions to specific types of cyberbullying.

4. Create an action plan for dealing with cyberbullying. This can include ignoring negative comments, recording and saving evidence, not engaging with the bully, blocking them to stop interactions, switching accounts to private, and reporting bullies to the website's administrator.

5. Discuss strategies teens find most useful.

DISCUSSION QUESTIONS

▶ What are some of the most popular ways bullies abuse the internet?

▶ How does technology make it easier for a bully to target people?

▶ Why is it important to know how to protect yourself online?

PRO TIPS

▶ Provide instructions on how to change privacy settings, block users, and report bullies on popular social media accounts.

▶ Give examples of assertive messages that can disengage the bully. For example, "You can call me whatever name you want, but it won't make you any better or make me any worse."

▶ Allow teens to lead the discussions, since they probably spend much more time on these internet outlets than you do.

Calling Out a Bully

Calling out a bully's behaviors to help protect others

Level 3
Becoming Bully-Proof

What You'll Need: Dry-erase board and markers

Duration: 25 to 35 minutes

Best for: 3 to 8 people

LEADING THE ACTIVITY

1. Ask the teens for examples of when they witnessed bullying and how they responded.

2. Reassure them that it can be difficult to know how to react when you see someone else being bullied.

3. Brainstorm ways to react when witnessing bullies. Write examples on the board.

4. Choose three volunteers and assign the following roles: bully, target, and witness.

5. Give teens a common bullying scenario that includes a witness stepping in to call out the bully. Allow them a few minutes to discuss the role-play.

6. Have them act out the scenario. After the witness calls out the bully, pause the action.

7. Choose another teen to be the witness. "Rewind" the role-play to a specific spot and let the new witness call out the bully.

8. Discuss the different approaches to calling out a bully.

DISCUSSION QUESTIONS

▶ Describe how you felt when you witnessed another person being bullied (in real life or during the role-plays).

▶ Which witnesses were most effective in calling out the bully? Why?

▶ How can standing up for someone being bullied make the situation better? Worse?

PRO TIPS

▶ As you substitute each new "witness" into the scenario, consider having the teens choose where to "rewind" to.

▶ To keep the role-plays respectful, set limits about what a bully can say or do.

CHAPTER 9

TRAUMA

Trauma is the mind and body's response to a deeply troubling experience. The symptoms of trauma may eventually go away on their own or lead to additional, longer-term symptoms, like flashbacks, unpredictable emotions, or a prolonged state of hypervigilance.

Using activities to treat trauma can be challenging. It's important to provide a safe, supportive environment that won't cause teens to be retraumatized. Before working with teens who have experienced significant trauma, specialized training is recommended. The following activities are meant to help teens address trauma while minimizing triggers and situations that may cause them to experience the trauma again.

The activities in this chapter are divided into three levels: Understanding Trauma (Level 1), How Trauma Affects Me (Level 2), and Healing from Trauma (Level 3). Level 1 activities give teens an overview of the topic to help identify sources of trauma. Level 2 activities help teens understand how trauma may be affecting their lives. Finally, Level 3 activities offer practical ways to address trauma and move forward.

Have I Experienced Trauma?

Understanding trauma and its common symptoms

Level 1
Understanding Trauma

What You'll Need: Dry-erase board and markers

Duration: 15 to 20 minutes

Best for: 3 to 8 people

LEADING THE ACTIVITY

1. Encourage the teens to provide their own definition of trauma.

2. Discuss types of traumatic events and have the group provide specific examples such as abuse and natural disasters. Write these on one side of the board.

3. Talk about some of the most common symptoms of trauma, such as nightmares, avoidance, and loss of interest in activities. Write the symptoms on another section of the board.

4. Describe some unfamiliar symptoms and ask the group to provide specific examples. Add these to the board.

5. Discuss ways to help deal with trauma, such as telling a trusted person, taking a self-assessment, joining a support group, and seeking help to deal with and manage symptoms.

DISCUSSION QUESTIONS

▶ What is something new you learned about trauma?

▶ If you think you're suffering from trauma, what is one thing you can do today to help yourself cope?

▶ Why is it important to understand the effects of trauma?

PRO TIPS

▶ Consider providing fact sheets about trauma.

▶ Discuss how symptoms of trauma often go away, especially with proper self-care and support.

▶ Be sure to remind teens trauma is not their fault. Blaming themselves will not help them cope.

Sharing My Story

Journaling to share traumatic experiences and start the healing process

What You'll Need: Pencils; paper; highlighters

Duration: 20 to 25 minutes

Best for: 1 person

Level 1
Understanding Trauma

LEADING THE ACTIVITY

1. Explain that traumatic experiences are often hard to talk about. Journaling can be a great way to sort out thoughts and emotions related to trauma.

2. Use the following prompts to guide the teen on a journaling experience regarding the trauma they experienced. Reassure the teen that they are completely in control of what they share. Allow 3 to 5 minutes for each writing prompt.

   - What are my present thoughts about the trauma I experienced?

   - What feelings am I holding on to about the trauma?

   - How do I think I can move away from these feelings?

   - Is my past trauma holding me back from living life?

   - Am I a stronger person now than I was before the trauma?

   - What have I learned about myself since experiencing the trauma?

3. When they are finished writing, encourage them to highlight parts of the journal entry they're willing to share.

DISCUSSION QUESTIONS

▶ Did writing about your trauma help? How?

▶ What insights did you have while journaling?

▶ How can sharing your trauma start the healing process?

PRO TIPS

▶ This activity works best if the facilitator has experience dealing with clients suffering from trauma.

▶ Journaling about a traumatic event can be very emotional for the teen. Provide support and encouragement.

▶ Validate whatever the teen is feeling and help them determine the next steps of their progress.

Trauma Isn't My Fault

Overcoming self-blame

Level 1
Understanding Trauma

What You'll Need: Dry-erase board and markers; small pieces of paper; pencils

Duration: 15 to 25 minutes

Best for: 3 to 8 people

LEADING THE ACTIVITY

1. Discuss how those struggling with trauma often blame themselves for their suffering. For example, a teen may believe it's their fault that they fell victim to a crime.

2. Have the group brainstorm additional ways people may blame themselves for something they had no control over. List the answers on the board.

3. Ask the teens to think about if and how they've blamed themselves for being involved in a traumatic experience. Allow them to reflect for a few minutes.

4. On small pieces of paper, have them write down some of the ways they currently or previously blamed themselves. Tell them their answers will be used as examples but will remain anonymous.

5. Collect the pieces of paper and shuffle.

6. Read each one aloud and discuss. Talk through each example to help the teens overcome self-blame.

DISCUSSION QUESTIONS

▶ Why do you think people blame themselves for traumatic experiences?

▶ What helpful insights did the group provide?

▶ How can being aware you're not at fault for your trauma help shift your perspective?

PRO TIPS

▶ While we want to help teens realize trauma isn't their fault, allow them to express any thoughts.

▶ Consider providing more examples of blaming oneself at the start of the activity.

▶ Allow the teens to arrive at their own conclusions and solutions.

Labeling Difficult Emotions

Exploring negative
emotions associated
with trauma

What You'll Need: Pencils and paper

Duration: 20 to 25 minutes

Best for: 1 to 6 people

Level 1
Understanding Trauma

LEADING THE ACTIVITY

1. Discuss the ways people who have experienced trauma often deal with difficult emotions. Explain that this is common but doesn't have to be permanent.

2. Talk about how labeling and describing different emotions can put feelings into better perspective and help with the healing process.

3. Ask the teen(s) to share any difficult thoughts or emotions associated with their trauma.

4. Explain that many feelings fall into three categories: shame, guilt, and anger.

5. Have the teen(s) divide a piece of paper into four sections—one for each of the three categories mentioned plus another for *Other/unsure*.

6. Ask them to place each of their trauma-related thoughts into one of the four categories.

7. Discuss and share only as they are comfortable.

DISCUSSION QUESTIONS

▶ Was it difficult to label your thoughts? Why or why not?

▶ How do you feel after taking a closer look at your thoughts and emotions?

▶ How can understanding typical thoughts and emotions associated with trauma help with the healing process?

PRO TIPS

▶ Encourage the teen(s) to go with their initial instinct when categorizing thoughts and emotions. If they are having trouble, they can put the thought in the *Other/ unsure* category.

▶ If they are not ready to share, let them provide a more generalized example.

▶ Teen(s) can take the paper home and fill in more thoughts and emotions over time.

Trauma Flashbacks

Understanding flashbacks and what may be causing them

What You'll Need: Pencils; paper; colored pencils or markers

Duration: 20 to 25 minutes

Best for: 1 person

Level 1
Understanding Trauma

LEADING THE ACTIVITY

1. Define **flashback** as a sudden and often disturbing memory of a past event. Explain that flashbacks are a common symptom of trauma.

2. Give the teen an overview of post-traumatic stress disorder (PTSD) and why flashbacks may occur.

3. Have them provide examples of flashbacks, either their own or ones they've witnessed.

4. Give them several moments to reflect on their flashbacks and answer any relevant questions.

5. Have them write, draw, or use any other form of creative expression to describe any flashbacks they've experienced. Tell them to include any warning signs or things that may trigger the flashback.

6. Discuss and share only as the teen is comfortable.

DISCUSSION QUESTIONS

▶ How often do you experience these flashbacks?

▶ Do certain triggers tend to cause the flashbacks?

▶ Why is it important to understand flashbacks?

PRO TIPS

▶ This activity is intended for those with a history of flashbacks.

▶ Be sure you understand how to help a teen experiencing a flashback in the event that this activity becomes a trigger.

▶ Provide tips for dealing with flashbacks at the end of the session.

My Trauma Triggers

Identifying trauma
triggers

Level 2
How Trauma Affects Me

What You'll Need: Pencils and paper

Duration: 20 to 25 minutes

Best for: 1 to 4 people

LEADING THE ACTIVITY

1. Discuss how certain people, situations, and stimuli can trigger symptoms of trauma. Explain that common trauma symptoms, such as avoidance, upsetting memories, and feeling emotionally numb, can negatively affect the healing process.

2. Ask the teen(s) to write down some common symptoms of their trauma in the middle of a piece of paper.

3. Around these symptoms, have them note some possible triggers. Then have them circle their most intense triggers or draw a star next to them.

4. Allow them to share their triggers and talk about which ones can and can't be avoided.

5. Discuss how to minimize triggers that can't be avoided.

DISCUSSION QUESTIONS

▶ What are your most common trauma triggers?

▶ What feelings or emotions come up most often when you feel triggered?

▶ How can understanding your triggers help with the healing process?

PRO TIPS

▶ Remind teen(s) that even simple things, like a light turning yellow at an intersection or a particular scent, may trigger symptoms of trauma.

▶ Discuss how working with a therapist can help reduce the effect of triggers over time.

Taking Back My Free Time

Discovering how trauma
impacts free time

Level 2
How Trauma Affects Me

What You'll Need: Pencils and paper

Duration: 20 to 25 minutes

Best for: 1 to 6 people

LEADING THE ACTIVITY

1. Discuss how struggling with trauma can keep us from doing the things we love.

2. On a piece of paper, have the teen(s) list their favorite leisure activities, including things they enjoyed doing in the past. Share and discuss.

3. Ask them to put a check mark next to activities they still do regularly and an "X" by activities they gave up or avoided since their traumatic event.

4. Discuss which activities were impacted most by trauma.

5. Ask them to come up with three actionable steps they can take in the next week to restart some of these activities.

6. Discuss.

DISCUSSION QUESTIONS

▶ What leisure activity do you miss the most? Why?

▶ What new leisure activities can you explore to help you focus on positive thoughts?

▶ Why do you think the choices you make during your free time can have an impact on your healing process?

PRO TIPS

▶ Ensure that teen(s) understand the concept of healthy leisure activities.

▶ Sometimes teens lose interest in previous leisure activities as time goes by. Ask them to determine whether trauma or something else caused them to lose interest in an activity.

▶ If necessary, dedicate the next session to find ways to revisit their favorite activities.

Catching Your Trauma

Exploring the impact
of trauma

Level 2
How Trauma Affects Me

What You'll Need: Large ball and marker

Duration: 15 to 25 minutes

Best for: 4 to 8 people

Prep: Write several questions related to the effects of trauma
on a large ball. For example, "How has trauma affected my
schoolwork?" Include enough questions so there's at least one
for each teen.

LEADING THE ACTIVITY

1. Have the group sit in a circle. Instruct them to catch the ball when it's thrown to
   them, answer whatever question is closest to their right thumb, and then throw
   the ball to another teen.

2. Throw the ball to one of the teens.

3. Repeat the process for the rest of the session.

4. Discuss the group's thoughts and insights the teens gained during the activity.

DISCUSSION QUESTIONS

▶ What did you learn from hearing your peers' answers?

▶ Which question did you dread answering the most? Why?

▶ How can talking about your trauma make it more manageable?

PRO TIPS

▶ To lighten things up a bit, consider adding some non-trauma questions to the ball,
  such as favorite food or music.

▶ To pass on answering a question, have the teen throw the ball to you and then provide them with another question.

Coping with Trauma

Exploring different ways to cope with trauma

Level 2
How Trauma Affects Me

What You'll Need: Dry-erase board and markers; sticky notes; pencils; tape

Duration: 20 to 30 minutes

Best for: 3 to 6 people

LEADING THE ACTIVITY

1. Acknowledge that dealing with the symptoms and effects of trauma can be very difficult.

2. Discuss positive and negative coping behaviors. Have teens give examples.

3. Hand out three to five sticky notes to each teen, and ask them to write one coping behavior on each note.

4. While they are writing, divide the board into two sections: positive coping and negative coping.

5. Collect the papers and shuffle.

6. Read each note out loud, keeping the answers anonymous. Have the group determine whether the behavior represents a positive or negative coping skill. Tape the notes to the appropriate section of the board.

7. Talk about ways to replace negative coping skills with positive ones.

8. Discuss the group's findings and progress.

DISCUSSION QUESTIONS

▶ What were some of the group's most common coping behaviors?

▶ Why do you think some people choose negative coping behaviors?

▶ How can finding positive ways to deal with symptoms of trauma help with the healing process?

PRO TIPS

▶ If the group is new to the concept of coping skills, define the phrase and discuss.

▶ Evaluate the coping behaviors without judging the actual person.

Thoughts That Weigh Me Down

Understanding how pessimistic thoughts impact our lives

Level 2
How Trauma Affects Me

What You'll Need: Small set of weights or another object to symbolize weights

Duration: 20 to 25 minutes

Best for: 3 to 8 people

LEADING THE ACTIVITY

1. Discuss how those struggling with trauma sometimes have pessimistic thoughts that weigh them down.

2. Define **pessimism** as a tendency to focus on the negative aspects of life. Discuss examples.

3. Explain how pessimism can lead to low motivation, depression, and hopelessness and may impact physical health.

4. Ask a volunteer to stand in front of the group and hold a small set of weights above their head. Instruct the teen to share a pessimistic thought that may be weighing them down.

5. As the teen continues to hold the weights, have the others call out more positive ways to see the situation.

6. Have the teen put weights down and take a deep breath. Ask them which tip they found most helpful.

7. Repeat the process with other volunteers.

DISCUSSION QUESTIONS

▶ Talk about a time you were struggling with pessimistic thoughts.

▶ What advice from the group resonated the most with you?

▶ How can learning to deal with pessimistic thoughts help your personal growth?

PRO TIPS

▶ Instead of using weights, the teen can simply write the pessimistic thought and hold it above their head.

▶ Make sure to thank volunteers for being brave and receiving feedback from the group.

Breathing through Difficult Moments

Feeling grounded in the face of difficult emotions

Level 3
Healing from Trauma

What You'll Need: No materials needed

Duration: 15 to 20 minutes

Best for: 1 to 4 people

LEADING THE ACTIVITY

1. Discuss how breathing exercises can help when we are overwhelmed with difficult emotions.

2. Ask the teen(s) to sit comfortably with their feet flat on the floor or stand tall and straight. Guide them through the following visualization:

   - Take a few deep breaths and close your eyes.

   - Imagine roots coming out of the bottom of your feet and pushing through the ground until they reach the center of the earth.

   - Now picture a bright light above your head.

   - As you breathe in, imagine that beam of light coming in through the top of your head and slowly working its way down your body.

   - Breathe out and feel your negative emotions sinking down through your feet, through the roots, and into the center of the earth.

   - Continue breathing in and out this way for a few minutes.

   - Now picture your body filled with this cleansing light, lifting your mood and energy.

   - Take a minute just to feel this light circulating through your body.

   - Now take a few deep breaths and slowly come back to the room.

DISCUSSION QUESTIONS

- ► Describe a situation when this activity can be helpful.
- ► How do you think grounding activities can help when you are faced with difficult emotions?

PRO TIPS

- ► Make sure the room has minimal distractions.
- ► Provide meaningful pauses between each step.
- ► Remind teen(s) that their minds will wander, and that is okay; they can just acknowledge it and return to the activity.

Five Senses Exercise

Getting grounded when overwhelmed by emotions

What You'll Need: No materials needed

Duration: 15 to 20 minutes

Best for: 1 to 6 people

Level 3
Healing from Trauma

LEADING THE ACTIVITY

1. Discuss how teens feel when overwhelmed with difficult emotions.

2. Explain that sometimes even simple activities can help "reset" the mind and make a person feel more grounded.

3. Guide teen(s) through the following exercise:

   - Hold up five fingers and name (out loud or to yourself) five things that you see.

   - Now hold up four fingers and name four things you touch.

   - Hold up three fingers and name three things you hear.

   - Hold up two fingers and name two things you smell.

   - Hold up one finger and name one thing you taste.

   - Now take a few deep breaths.

4. Repeat the exercise to help them remember it.

DISCUSSION QUESTIONS

▶ How did you feel before this activity? Afterward?

▶ Name a specific time when you feel this activity would be helpful.

▶ How can learning to stay grounded help you when you experience difficult emotions?

PRO TIPS

▶ This exercise works better with practice. Have teen(s) practice this from time to time so it can be more useful when they really need it.

▶ This is also a great short exercise that can be included in other sessions—especially if teen(s) are getting anxious or unruly.

▶ If time allows, have teen(s) create an illustration of this exercise as a visual reminder to use this technique.

Building My Support System

Creating concrete plans
to ask for help during
difficult times

What You'll Need: Pencils and paper

Duration: 20 to 25 minutes

Best for: 1 to 5 people

Level 3
Healing from Trauma

LEADING THE ACTIVITY

1. Discuss how having a support system is very important for teens struggling
   with trauma. The feelings and symptoms of trauma can be overwhelming, so it is
   important to have sources of help readily available.

2. Have the teen(s) list five people or resources they can go to when they are having
   a bad day.

3. Next to each person or resource, have the teen(s) write why they chose them and
   how they can help.

4. Then have them write a clear statement about when they would reach out to each
   person or resource. For example, "When I feel like harming myself, I can call ..."

5. Discuss the importance of having allies and a strong support system.

DISCUSSION QUESTIONS

▶ Was it difficult to come up with five trusted people and resources? Why or
   why not?

▶ Describe a time when you felt like you really needed to reach out to someone.

▶ In what ways can a support system help you recover from trauma?

PRO TIPS

▶ Consider providing a list of local resources and phone numbers that teen(s) can
   easily access.

▶ If time permits, allow the teen(s) to identify negative people and places in their life
   that can make bad days worse.

▶ Guide teen(s) to make their statements clear and actionable, like a set of instructions
   to themselves.

Reflecting on My Trauma

Reframing trauma to
shift perspective

What You'll Need: Pencils and paper

Duration: 20 to 30 minutes

Level 3
Healing from Trauma

Best for: 1 to 4 people

LEADING THE ACTIVITY

1. Discuss how reframing the way we look at trauma can be an important step in the recovery process. For example, someone who suffered a bad accident may develop a greater appreciation for the simpler pleasures of life.

2. Give the teen(s) a few minutes to write down some learning experiences and life lessons that resulted from their trauma.

3. Allow them to share.

4. Encourage them to recognize that they have become stronger by surviving their trauma and taking brave steps to heal.

5. Give the teen(s) time to journal their thoughts on the following prompt: "I am stronger because of what I've been through."

6. Allow them to share what they've journaled as they feel comfortable.

DISCUSSION QUESTIONS

▶ What important lessons do you feel your trauma taught you?

▶ How can reframing your experience help you start the healing process?

▶ How can referring back to what you wrote during this activity help you on difficult days?

PRO TIPS

▶ This activity is best for one-on-one sessions or a group that already has good rapport.

▶ Writing about these experiences can bring up difficult emotions. After they have journaled, be sure to provide emotional support and consider using some of the grounding exercises described earlier in the chapter.

▶ Congratulate the teen(s) for taking the first steps to begin healing from trauma.

Portrait of Recovery

Visualizing successful
recovery from trauma

Level 3
Healing from Trauma

What You'll Need: Pencils; paper; colored pencils; markers; old magazines, images printed from the internet, or any other available art material

Duration: 30 to 40 minutes

Best for: 1 to 5 people

LEADING THE ACTIVITY

1. Acknowledge that the teen(s) have been through a lot already in their lives.

2. Discuss what changes they would like to see from this day forward. What activities would they like to experience, feelings they want to overcome, new personal habits they'd like to develop?

3. Allow the teen(s) to create a portrait of how they want their recovery to look. It can be concrete or abstract, using words, drawings, images from magazines—whatever they choose. It is simply a time to creatively focus on recovery.

4. Allow them to present their artwork and discuss their goals for recovery.

DISCUSSION QUESTIONS

▶ What do you like best about your artwork?

▶ What thoughts or emotions came up while you were creating your portrait?

▶ What can you start doing today to make your image a reality?

PRO TIPS

▶ Provide as many different art materials as possible to engage the teen(s).

▶ Offer positive feedback or ideas if a teen is struggling to complete the portrait.

▶ Reassure them that there are no right or wrong ways to complete this activity.

CHAPTER 10

GRIEF

Grief is our natural reaction to the sudden loss of a loved one or other major change in life. Grief can feel overwhelming, especially for teens who have difficulty expressing their thoughts and emotions.

The grieving process is different for everyone. Experts have identified milestones that can occur during the process, but there is no exact timeline or progression for grieving. Everyone experiences grief in different ways. The activities in this chapter give teens a chance to express their sense of loss and learn how to move on to face their new reality.

The activities in this chapter are divided into three levels: Understanding Grief (Level 1), Managing Grief (Level 2), and Working through Grief (Level 3). Level 1 activities give teens a chance to take a closer look at their loss and how it is affecting them. Level 2 activities give practical approaches to help teens deal with grief. Finally, Level 3 activities allow a teen to take the first brave steps in moving past their grief.

Grief in My Own Words

Finding a personal
definition of grief

Level 1
Understanding Grief

What You'll Need: Pencils and paper

Duration: 15 to 20 minutes

Best for: 1 to 6 people

LEADING THE ACTIVITY

1. Acknowledge that the teen(s) are going through some form of grief. Ask them how familiar they are with the grief process.

2. Provide a definition of grief as pain or sorrow that often accompanies a sudden major loss.

3. Allow teen(s) to provide their own definition of grief based on their experience.

4. Briefly discuss each of the seven stages of grief: shock or disbelief, denial, bargaining, guilt, anger, depression, and acceptance/hope.

5. Have teen(s) write what each of these stages means to them.

6. Ask for volunteers to share their examples.

DISCUSSION QUESTIONS

▶ What has this session taught you about grief?

▶ Were there any stages of grief you had difficulty writing about?

▶ How can understanding grief and the grief process help you with what you're currently feeling?

PRO TIPS

▶ If a teen has difficulty coming up with a definition of grief, allow them to just write a couple of words that describe what they are going through.

▶ Remind them that the grief process is not necessarily linear; individuals experience the stages in different ways.

▶ If time allows, have the teen(s) pick their favorite definitions of grief and write them on a dry-erase board (if you have one available).

What Grief Feels Like

Developing an expanded emotional vocabulary to describe feelings around grief

Level 1
Understanding Grief

What You'll Need: Pencils; list of emotions associated with grief

Duration: 15 to 20 minutes

Best for: 1 to 5 people

Prep: Create a list of emotions associated with grief and make a copy for each participant.

LEADING THE ACTIVITY

1. Acknowledge that emotions related to grief are difficult and sometimes hard to explain.

2. Discuss how becoming more aware of different emotions can help the teen(s) come to terms with grief.

3. Ask the teen(s) to describe a time when they had difficulty expressing how they felt about their loss.

4. Provide them with the list of emotions.

5. Review the list and ask them to define each word or provide examples.

6. Then give them a few minutes to circle all the emotions they have experienced in their grief.

7. Provide time for sharing and discussion.

DISCUSSION QUESTIONS

▶ What emotions do you most associate with grief?

▶ Did this activity help you communicate what you are feeling? How?

▶ How can identifying your emotions help you better understand your grief?

PRO TIPS

▶ Lists of emotions are easily found on the internet.

▶ Before you provide the list, consider having the teen(s) brainstorm emotions related to grief.

▶ Reassure them that there are no right or wrong answers; everyone experiences grief differently.

Survivor's Guilt

Identifying and understanding thoughts and feelings associated with survivor's guilt

What You'll Need: Pencils; paper; colored pencils or markers

Duration: 20 to 25 minutes

Best for: 1 to 3 people

Level 1
Understanding Grief

LEADING THE ACTIVITY

1. Define **survivor's guilt**, an intense emotion or feeling that it is unfair for someone to have survived a trauma or catastrophic event when others didn't.

2. Discuss some of the common symptoms of survivor's guilt.

3. Instruct the teen(s) to create an image of themselves struggling with survivor's guilt. Tell them they can depict this in any way they choose.

4. Around the image, have them create thought bubbles and fill them with thoughts related to their survivor's guilt.

5. Allow them to share some thoughts and discuss.

DISCUSSION QUESTIONS

▶ What have you learned about survivor's guilt?

▶ Why do you think survivors feel guilty after a traumatic event?

▶ How can understanding survivor's guilt help guide you through the grief process?

PRO TIPS

▶ Not everyone going through grief will experience survivor's guilt. Ensure that this activity is appropriate for your teen(s).

▶ This activity is best for a one-on-one session or for a small group of teens who have been through similar situations.

▶ Provide encouragement but respect a teen's decision to share or not.

It's Okay to Laugh

Working through grief's
difficult emotions
with laughter

What You'll Need: Pencils and paper; internet access
(if possible)

Duration: 25 to 35 minutes

Level 1
Understanding Grief

Best for: 3 to 6 people

LEADING THE ACTIVITY

1. Ask the teens if they feel guilty for laughing or having fun while they are still grieving.

2. Explain that it is okay to laugh and that it can help with the healing process.

3. Clarify that laughter is not a sign of disrespect nor does it minimize the impact of one's loss. Rather, it's a chance to embrace the moment and begin to move on while still remembering your loved one.

4. Ask them to think of 10 things that make them laugh, like a joke, an internet video, or a memory.

5. Have them discuss their answers and share what made them laugh.

6. To encourage the group to laugh, play some funny videos if possible.

7. Discuss why laughter is important during difficult times.

DISCUSSION QUESTIONS

▶ Name one of the funniest things mentioned in the group.

▶ How did it feel to laugh today?

▶ Why does taking time to laugh help with the grieving process?

PRO TIPS

▶ When appropriate, ask the teens to mention a few things about their lost loved one that made them laugh.

▶ Let the discussion move freely, as the teens may come up with additional things that make them laugh.

▶ Using media during this activity is a great way for teens to laugh together.

Before and After

Identifying feelings before and after a significant loss

Level 1
Understanding Grief

What You'll Need: Pencils and paper; dry-erase board and markers

Duration: 20 to 25 minutes

Best for: 1 to 4 people

LEADING THE ACTIVITY

1. Discuss how a traumatic incident like a loved one's passing can change a person's mind-set and world view.

2. Instruct the teen(s) to draw a line down the middle of a piece of paper.

3. On the left side of the paper, have them write feelings and thoughts they recall having about the loved one before their death. Provide a few minutes for quiet reflection.

4. On the right side of the paper, have them write feelings and thoughts they have experienced about the loved one after their passing. Provide a few minutes for quiet reflection.

5. Allow them to share (if comfortable) and discuss how the traumatic event changed their mind-set—for example, feeling insecure about the future or fear of experiencing a similar fate.

DISCUSSION QUESTIONS

▶ What was the biggest change in your mind-set after your loved one's passing?

▶ What thoughts and feelings do you wish you could get back? Why?

▶ How does recognizing your thoughts and feelings after a loved one's passing help with the grieving process?

PRO TIPS

▶ This is best for a one-on-one session or with a small group of teens with similar experiences.

▶ Validate thoughts without trying to change them. This is an exploratory activity.

▶ This activity may bring up intense emotions; make sure you have training to support those who are grieving.

Grieving Creatively

Focusing on positive thoughts and emotions through creativity

Level 2
Managing Grief

What You'll Need: Paper; pencils; markers; paints; colored pencils; scissors; glue; old magazines

Duration: 20 to 30 minutes

Best for: 1 to 6 people

LEADING THE ACTIVITY

1. Discuss how engaging in leisure activities can help shift your focus away from strong negative emotions related to grief.

2. Provide available art materials. Allow teen(s) time to create artwork. There doesn't have to be a theme—just let the teen(s) immerse themselves in the activity.

3. Have them share their artwork and discuss what they made.

4. Discuss feelings or thoughts that occurred while they were completing the artwork.

DISCUSSION QUESTIONS

▶ Did you encounter any negative feelings while creating your artwork? How did continuing your artwork help you refocus?

▶ What did you like best about this activity?

▶ How can finding activities that resonate with you help shift your focus during difficult times?

PRO TIPS

▶ Introduce the concept of **flow**, which is when an activity becomes so engaging that they lose track of time and self while completing it. Discuss how activities that put them in the flow state can help shift moods.

▶ Encourage teen(s) to create without any expectations. Their artwork doesn't have to be about grief.

▶ Provide a variety of art materials so that teen(s) can find a medium that resonates with them.

Staying Healthy After Loss

Using moderate exercise to improve one's mood and remain healthy while struggling with grief

Level 2
Managing Grief

What You'll Need: Open area; music player; dry-erase board and markers

Duration: 15 to 25 minutes

Best for: 3 to 8 people

LEADING THE ACTIVITY

1. Discuss how emotions related to grief can make a person feel unfocused, unmotivated, and depressed.

2. Introduce physical exercise as a way to help regain energy and focus and feel better overall.

3. Brainstorm some of the group's favorite exercises, to be incorporated into a short routine. Write them on the board.

4. If necessary, add a few simple exercises to the list.

5. Have the teens create an 8- to 10-minute routine using these exercises.

6. Play some music and guide them through the routine.

7. Discuss how exercise helped change their mood and mind-set.

DISCUSSION QUESTIONS

▶ How do you feel after completing the exercise routine?

▶ How many physical activities do you do a week?

▶ How can incorporating exercise into your daily routine help with your mood and ability to deal with difficult emotions?

PRO TIPS

▶ Ensure that the exercise routine is inclusive to everyone in the group.

▶ Ask them to come to this session wearing comfortable clothes, if possible.

▶ The more the teens collaborate on the exercise routine, the more likely they will be to complete it.

Self-Care Schedule

Exploring different self-care options to manage grief

Level 2
Managing Grief

What You'll Need: Dry-erase board and markers; pencils; paper

Duration: 20 to 30 minutes

Best for: 1 to 6 people

LEADING THE ACTIVITY

1. Ask the teen(s) to define self-care as activities people do intentionally to care for their mental, emotional, and physical well-being. Give examples.

2. Discuss that self-care plays a big role in working through difficult times.

3. Write the following categories on the board: *Physical movement, Soothing or relaxing activities, Rest, Creative expression, Eating healthy,* and *Mindfulness/ meditation.*

4. Have the teen(s) brainstorm self-care activities for each of the categories.

5. On a piece of paper, have them create a weekly schedule of self-care, with specific times designated for activities each day. Encourage them to practice self-care for at least 15 minutes a day.

6. Share and discuss their schedules.

DISCUSSION QUESTIONS

▸ What are some of your favorite self-care activities?

▸ What are some new self-care activities you discovered today?

▸ How can scheduling self-care activities on specific days and times help you follow through with the schedule?

PRO TIPS

▸ Consider providing examples of self-care and having the teen(s) determine the appropriate categories.

▸ If they are having trouble coming up with self-care activities, provide a list for them.

▸ On the schedule, have teen(s) write what they are usually doing before and after the allotted times for self-care.

You're Not Alone

Identifying people who
can help through the
grief process

Level 2
Managing Grief

What You'll Need: Pencils and paper

Duration: 20 to 25 minutes

Best for: 2 to 6 people

LEADING THE ACTIVITY

1. Discuss the importance of getting support while working through the grieving process.

2. Have the teens give a few examples of people who make up their support network. Ask why they chose these people.

3. On a piece of paper, have them list at least five people they can ask for help.

4. Next to each person, have them write what makes these people supportive. For example, "My sister always takes the time to listen when I'm feeling down."

5. Then ask them to write down specific days and times each person is typically available.

6. Allow the teens to discuss the schedule.

7. Instruct them to use their lists as a resource when they are having a difficult time managing grief.

DISCUSSION QUESTIONS

▸ What were some of the main reasons you chose the people for your list?

▸ How likely are you to reach out to these people in times of need?

▸ Are there any days or times when you don't have access to support? How can you fill this gap?

PRO TIPS

▸ If necessary, provide a list of resources teens could reach out to when friends and family aren't available.

▸ To give the teens more ideas for their support network, discuss the different ways other people can help with the grief process.

▸ If time allows, have the teens create a weekly calendar and highlight times they have available support.

Grief Takes Time

Identifying challenges and celebrating successes in the grieving process

What You'll Need: Pencils and paper

Duration: 20 to 25 minutes

Best for: 1 to 6 people

Level 2
Managing Grief

LEADING THE ACTIVITY

1. Explain that the grieving process takes time. Everyone experiences it differently, and there is no exact timeline.

2. Allow the teen(s) to discuss their thoughts about the grief process.

3. Have each teen divide a piece of paper in half and label one side *Moving forward* and the other *My challenges*.

4. On the *Moving forward* side, have them write about the progress they've made since their loss.

5. On the *My challenges* side, have them write about difficulties they've experienced since their loss.

6. Allow them to share their progress and challenges.

7. Encourage the teen(s) to celebrate their successes since the loss and use them as motivation to help confront their challenges.

DISCUSSION QUESTIONS

▶ What is your biggest win so far working through the grieving process?

▶ What challenges are you most afraid to confront? Why?

▶ How can building on your successes help ease the burden of working through grief?

PRO TIPS

▶ Remind the teen(s) that no success is too small. Every little step moves them forward in the healing process.

▶ If necessary, prompt teen(s) as they write about each category, especially the *Moving forward* section. For example, "How have you adjusted since your loss?"

▶ If time allows, let them brainstorm ways they can confront their challenges.

My Grief Journal

Learning how journaling can help with the grief process

Level 3
Working through Grief

What You'll Need: Small notebooks; pencils; dry-erase board and markers

Duration: 25 to 30 minutes

Best for: 1 to 4 people

LEADING THE ACTIVITY

1. Ask the teen(s) about their favorite ways to express emotions—negative and positive.

2. Introduce journaling as an option for working through grief.

3. Give each teen a small notebook that will serve as their journal.

4. Brainstorm some journaling topics that serve as good starting points, such as "my daily check-in" and "how to keep good memories alive." Write these on the board.

5. Explain that journaling is an individual process—an opportunity to write whatever thoughts or feelings they need to express. The journal doesn't have to be shared with anyone.

6. Allow 10 to 15 minutes for their first journaling session. They can pick a topic on the board or another if they prefer.

7. Have the teen(s) talk about how it felt to express their thoughts and emotions through writing.

DISCUSSION QUESTIONS

▶ How did it feel to put some of your thoughts and feelings on paper?

▶ What are some other journaling topics you want to write about?

▶ How do you plan to use this journal in the future?

PRO TIPS

▶ Consider taking a few minutes to discuss the benefits of journaling before starting the activity.

▶ Remind the teen(s) that there is no right or wrong way to journal.

▶ Allow different ways to journal, like doodling, making lists, or creating a poem.

Memory Box

Creating a memory box
to honor a lost loved one

Level 3
Working through Grief

What You'll Need: Old shoeboxes or similar sized boxes;
any available art materials; quotes about overcoming grief

Duration: 25 to 35 minutes

Best for: 1 to 5 people

LEADING THE ACTIVITY

1. Talk about the importance of honoring a lost loved one and brainstorm ways the teen(s) can do this.

2. Introduce them to the concept of a memory box: a decorated box where they can store reminders of the person they lost. It can contain pictures, letters, small gifts or mementos, a list of quotes, or anything else that helps keep the memory alive.

3. Give the teen(s) 10 to 15 minutes to decorate their memory box in any way they choose.

4. Then allow them to display the box and discuss the decorations they chose.

5. Ask them about specific items they want to place in the memory box.

DISCUSSION QUESTIONS

▶ What made you choose to decorate your memory box in that way?

▶ Name three things you intend to put in the memory box.

▶ How can keeping a memory box honor your loved one and help you manage grief?

PRO TIPS

▶ Shoeboxes or boxes that are a little larger tend to work best.

▶ Provide as many art materials as possible so teen(s) have different creative options.

▶ This activity works best for teen(s) who have already taken steps to work through their grief with some of the previous activities and supplemental counseling.

Talking to Peers

Weighing the pros and cons of discussing grief with peers

Level 3
Working through Grief

What You'll Need: Dry-erase board and markers

Duration: 20 to 30 minutes

Best for: 2 to 6 people

Prep: Create a list of local resources and peer groups where teens can discuss their grief, and make copies for all participants.

LEADING THE ACTIVITY

1. Explain that the grieving process often requires reaching out to others for support and assistance. Ask the teens to name people they'd feel comfortable talking to about their grief.

2. Discuss what it might be like to discuss their grief with peers.

3. Acknowledge that peers can be very supportive, but some may not have experienced the same sort of grief.

4. Have them brainstorm the pros and cons of discussing their grief with peers. Write their ideas on the board.

5. Discuss how seeking professional help as well as the support of peers may be the best way to work through grief.

6. Provide the list of local resources and peer groups.

DISCUSSION QUESTIONS

▶ What are some ways your peers have supported you through your grief?

▶ Describe a time when you felt you needed more than peer support.

▶ How can talking to both trusted peers and professionals help you work through grief?

PRO TIPS

▶ If time allows, have the teens role-play scenarios where peers give good support and others where they may make a person feel worse.

▶ Encourage the teens to list three friends who they find most supportive.

Writing a Letter

Expressing feelings while addressing the source of grief

Level 3
Working through Grief

What You'll Need: Pencils; paper; envelopes

Duration: 20 to 30 minutes

Best for: 1 to 4 people

LEADING THE ACTIVITY

1. Discuss how losing a loved one often results in intense and difficult-to-express emotions.

2. Allow the teen(s) to discuss some of the difficult times they have faced.

3. Ask them to write a letter to help put some of their most difficult emotions into words. It can be addressed to the lost loved one, God, a higher power, or even themselves.

4. Give the teen(s) 10 to 15 minutes to write the letter. Reassure them that they only need to share if they are comfortable.

5. When they're finished, ask if they feel comfortable sharing any part of the letter. Remind them it is perfectly fine to keep it private.

6. Have them seal the letter in an envelope. Tell them to keep it wherever they wish.

7. Discuss how they felt when writing down their feelings.

DISCUSSION QUESTIONS

- ▶ What emotions did you experience while writing the letter?
- ▶ Did writing the letter make you feel better or worse? How?
- ▶ How can writing help you move on from your experience of loss?

PRO TIPS

- ▶ Writing this letter may be an emotional experience. Provide support when necessary.
- ▶ Assure the teen(s) that anything they write, or feel while writing, is perfectly fine for the moment. This is their opportunity to purge built-up emotions.
- ▶ Consider ending the session with a short visualization activity where they imagine handing the letter to their intended recipient. Suggest that this is a time they can let go of the difficult emotions they wrote about.

Letting Go

Letting go of crippling
thoughts and feelings
related to grief

What You'll Need: No materials needed

Duration: 20 to 25 minutes

Best for: 1 to 4 people

Level 3
Working through Grief

LEADING THE ACTIVITY

1. Discuss how losing a loved one may make it difficult to let go of certain thoughts and emotions.

2. Explain that "letting go" doesn't mean forgetting the person or diminishing their role in your life. It is just a part of the grieving process.

3. With the teen(s) seated comfortably, guide them through the following visualization:

   - Imagine you are holding a large balloon.

   - Now imagine filling it with feelings, emotions, regrets, or bad memories to let go of.

   - Watch it slowly expand.

   - Take a close look at it and say to the balloon, "I am now ready to let go."

   - Imagine letting go of the balloon. Watch it slowly float into the sky until it disappears.

   - Say to yourself, "I have now let go." Feel yourself become lighter, less burdened, and more able to face the day.

   - Whenever you struggle with these feelings again, take a moment to think of that balloon disappearing in the sky. Say to yourself, "I've already let go."

   - Take a few deep breaths and feel yourself coming back into the room.

4. Give the teen(s) a chance to discuss how they felt during this activity.

DISCUSSION QUESTIONS

▶ How did you feel during and after this visualization?

▶ Do you think it's okay to let go of the thoughts and emotions you put in the balloon? Why or why not?

▶ How can symbolically letting go be a first step in releasing painful thoughts and emotions?

PRO TIPS

▶ This activity is best for teen(s) who have completed previous activities on managing grief.

▶ Teen(s) can use the image of the balloon disappearing to help refocus their mind when they are overcome with emotions.

▶ You can substitute other metaphors for the balloon, such attaching thoughts to a heavy rock and throwing it into the sea.

Resources

Here are some resources you can use and explore to learn more about teen mental health issues, and to find inspiration for your activity planning.

Websites

The American Psychological Association (APA.org) provides an informative page to help teachers and other professionals understand how to work with children and teens dealing with trauma.

Grow Through Flow (GrowThroughFlow.com) is another great blog written by a professional with lots of sound mental health tips and advice for self-care and caring for others.

HEARD Alliance (HEARDAlliance.org) is a place for professionals and families to access and use resources that promote well-being, prevent suicide, and treat depression and other related conditions in adolescents and young adults.

MentalHealth.gov is a great starting point for parents and professionals to get education and guidance regarding mental health issues.

My Recreation Therapist (MyRecreationTherapist.com) helps connect recreation therapists with private clients.

The National Child Traumatic Stress Network (NCTSN.org) offers a page with several fact sheets and tips to help teens recover from traumatic events.

Recreation Therapy Ideas (RecTherapyIdeas.blogspot.com) is an older blog with lots of relevant ideas for developing your therapy groups.

RT Wise Owls (Sites.Temple.edu/rtwiseowls) is a free database and information resource center developed by the Recreational Therapy (RT) program at Temple University.

Social Workers Toolbox (SocialWorkersToolbox.com) offers free social work tools and resources covering a variety of topics.

StopBullying.gov is a website created by the US government to address, prevent, and stop all forms of bullying.

Therapeutic Recreation Directory (RecreationTherapy.com) offers a variety of resources and activity ideas for recreation therapists.

Therapist Aid (TherapistAid.com) offers several resources, worksheets, and interactive experiences for mental health professionals.

Organizations

American Therapeutic Recreation Association (ATRA-Online.com) is the only national membership organization representing and empowering the needs of recreation therapists.

National Council for Therapeutic Recreation Certification (NCTRC.org) is the website for the credentialing organization for the profession of Therapeutic Recreation.

Books

Sagamore Venture Publishing (SagamorePub.com) offers educational materials for leisure education, recreation therapy, outdoor recreation, and other related topics.

Continuing Education

Rec Therapy Today (RecTherapyToday.com) offers self-study Continuing Education Units (CEU) programs, courses, workshops, and webinars to renew certification through NCTRC and/or state licenses.

SMART CEUs Hub (SmartCEUsHub.com) is a resource for recreation therapist continuing education, including unlimited yearly subscriptions and individual courses.

Index